Mary and Joseph, and Other Dialogue Poems on Mary

Texts from Christian Late Antiquity

8

Series Editor
George Anton Kiraz

TeCLA (Texts from Christian Late Antiquity) is a new series presenting ancient Christian texts both in their original languages and with accompanying contemporary English translations.

Mary and Joseph, and Other Dialogue Poems on Mary

Sebastian P. Brock

gorgias press
2011

Gorgias Press LLC, 954 River Road, Piscataway, NJ, 08854, USA

www.gorgiaspress.com

Copyright © 2011 by Gorgias Press LLC

All rights reserved under International and Pan-American Copyright Conventions. No part of this publication may be reproduced, stored in a retrieval system or transmitted in any form or by any means, electronic, mechanical, photocopying, recording, scanning or otherwise without the prior written permission of Gorgias Press LLC.

2011

ISBN 978-1-59333-839-8   ISSN 1935-6846

Library of Congress Cataloging-in-Publication Data
Mary and Joseph, and other dialogue poems on Mary / [compiled] by Sebastian P. Brock.
    p. cm. -- (Texts from Christian late antiquity, ISSN 1935-6846 ; 8)
  Includes bibliographical references and indexes.
  1. Mary, Blessed Virgin, Saint--Poetry. 2. Christian poetry, Syriac. I. Brock, Sebastian P.
   PJ5617.M37 2011
   892'.3--dc22

2011007425

Printed in the United States of America

TABLE OF CONTENTS

Introduction 1
Syriac Introduction 7

Texts and Translations 9
    I. Mary and the Angel 9
    II. Mary and Joseph 31
    III. Mary and the Magi 49
    IV–V. Mary and the Gardener 69
    IV. Mary and the Gardener (East Syriac poem) 70
    V. Mary and the Gardener (West Syriac poem) 76

Annotation 87
    Abbreviations 87
    I. Mary and the Angel 87
    II. Mary and Joseph 89
    III. Mary and the Magi 89
    IV–V. Mary and the Gardener 90

Select Bibliography 93
    (a) Dialogue and dispute poems 93
    (b) Mary in Syriac tradition 93

Appendix: Dialogue *Sughyotho* 97
    Old Testament 97
    New Testament 98
    Other topics (in alphabetical order) 101
    (a) Personifications 101
    (b) Individuals 103

Index of Names and Themes 105
Index of Biblical References 107

INTRODUCTION

One of the most distinctive literary genres in Syriac is that of the dialogue poem in which two characters (who may also be personifications) conduct and argument in short alternating verses. The earliest examples of this type of poem are to be found among Ephrem's Nisibene *Madroshe* (nos. 52–54), where Death and Satan argue over which of the two has more power over human beings. Ephrem has in fact adapted a very ancient Mesopotamian literary genre to a new context, for precedence disputes of this sort can be traced back at least to the second millennium BC, composed in Sumerian and Akkadian. Examples closer in time to Ephrem are to be found in Jewish Aramaic and in Middle Persian. Subsequently the genre was taken up in both Modern Persian and Arabic, and it has clearly continued to be a popular one right up to the present day, for examples have been collected in both Modern Syriac and in Modern Arabic dialects.[1]

In Syriac the precedence element still features in a certain number of these dialogue poems, but more frequently it is replaced by an argument with a specifically religious concern; this not surprisingly applies above all to the many dialogues in which the protagonists are biblical characters, and very frequently the underlying issue concerns the conflicting demands of reason and faith. The arguments are conducted in a lively and highly imaginative and realistic way. A particularly notable example of this is provided by the second dialogue in this collection, where Joseph, arriving home to find his fiancée pregnant, not unnaturally assumes that she has been unfaithful and accordingly rebukes her sharply; only very gradually does poor Mary manage to persuade him that there might be some truth in her initial reply to him, that 'a man of fire came down, he gave me a greeting, and this took place'.

---

[1] Further information can be found in the general surveys in Murray 1995 and Brock 2001 (for the titles, see the Select Bibliography).

In the majority of the dialogue poems on biblical topics, the dialogue takes as its starting point a single moment in the biblical narrative (such as Joseph's discovery that Mary is pregnant, Matthew 1:18), and then imaginatively explores what the reactions of the characters involved might have been. In a few instances only one of the speakers is actually mentioned in the biblical text: this is the case with the dialogue between the repentant Thief of Luke 23:40–43 and the Cherub. In this *sughitho*, which has remained a popular one over the centuries, the second speaker is the Cherub who is guarding Paradise (Genesis 3:24), and whose instructions are to keep human beings out; accordingly, when the Thief turns up, confident in Jesus's promise to him that 'today you shall be with me in Paradise', the Cherub tenaciously bars his entry, and it is only when the Thief eventually produces the Cross that the Cherub finally allows him to enter:

> This Cross of the Son which you've brought to me
> is something I don't dare look upon at all.
> It is both genuine and awesome: no longer will you be debarred
> from entering Eden, seeing that He has so willed it.

Likewise, in the Dialogue between Satan and the Sinful Woman, where the episode is based on Luke 7:37, Satan is never mentioned in the Gospel narrative. What the anonymous author has done here is to exteriorize, as it were, in the person of Satan, all the inner doubts and hesitation which the woman must have felt before boldly entering the house of an important person who was a complete stranger in order to anoint the feet of that man's principal guest.[2]

That five different dialogue poems should be concerned with Mary is no surprise, given the high regard and honour with which she is held in all the Syriac Churches. The three oldest dialogue poems in which she is a speaker are all based on episodes in the Infancy Narratives of the Gospels of Matthew and Luke, the Annunciation (Luke 1:26–37), Joseph's discovery of her pregnancy (Matthew 1:18), and the Visit of the Magi (Matthew 2:10–11). Liturgically, they all belong to the Sundays leading up to, and immediately following the Nativity. In both the East and West Syriac liturgical traditions the Sundays before the Nativity are known as the Period of the *Suboro*, or Annunciation, with successive Sundays devoted to (in the Syrian Orthodox Calendar) the Annunciation of Zechariah (Luke 1:8–23), the An-

---

[2] For the translations available for these two poems, and for the other biblical topics covered, see the Appendix.

nunciation to Mary, the Visit of Elizabeth to Mary (Luke 1:39–56), the Birth of John the Baptist (Luke 1:57–66), and the Revelation to Joseph (Matthew 1:20–21). Only in the West Syriac tradition,[3] and probably not until at least the sixth century, did a separate Feast of the Annunciation on March 25th get introduced, as well.

The last two poems in this collection are based on the Resurrection narrative of John 20:11–17, and both identify the Mary of these verses as Mary, the mother of Jesus, distinguishing this Mary from Mary Magdalene, who is specifically mentioned in John 20:1 and 18. In doing this, the anonymous authors of these two poems follow an early, and quite widespread, tradition that the risen Christ also appeared to his mother.[4] It is interesting to note that it was the Resurrection narrative of John 20 which gave rise to the earliest hints of liturgical drama in the medieval West. There, it took several centuries before a fully fledged liturgical drama emerged, around the twelfth century, in France. Although some scholars have seen hints of the existence of liturgical drama also in the Greek East, as far as the Syriac tradition is concerned, the nearest thing to liturgical drama that one finds is in the dialogue between the Cherub and the Thief, which, traditionally, is performed in church in a stylised fashion, with the actions of the two protagonists mimed by deacons.[5]

*

Most of the fifty or so dialogue poems that are at present known are anonymous. Those that are transmitted in both the Eastern and Western Syriac manuscript traditions are likely to belong approximately to the fifth century, while those preserved only in one tradition are likely to come from

---

[3] That is Syrian Orthodox, Maronite, and Rum Orthodox (Melkite) for whom Syriac continued in some areas as a liturgical language until the early eighteenth century. In the East Syriac tradition the Feast of the Annunciation on March 25th has been introduced in the Chaldean Catholic Church. All the Syriac Churches have a special Feast devoted to Mary immediately after the Nativity.

[4] The West Syriac poem (no. V) perhaps dates from the early centuries of Arab rule, while the presence of end rhyme in the East Syriac one (no. IV) points to a later date (my earlier suggestion, in the *editio princeps*, of the possibility of a sixth-century date, should be dropped).

[5] A colourful description of this is given by W. A. Wigram in his *The Assyrians and their Neighbours*, 198. London, 1929 (quoted in Brock 1984, p. 47). On this topic, see further "Seeds of liturgical drama in Syriac?" In Chehwan, A., and A. Kassis, eds. *Mélanges offerts au P. Féghali*, 323–41. Dekouaneh, 2002.

later centuries. In the East Syriac tradition quite a number of the dialogue poems are transmitted under the name of Narsai, but this attribution is not likely to be correct. Among the latest will be those by 'Abdisho' of Soba (Nisibis),[6] who died in 1318, and by Khamis bar Qarda<u>h</u>e (13th/14th century). The dialogue poems are regularly described as *sughyotho* (a term which covers much more than just the dialogue poems), and very frequently there is also an alphabetic acrostic present, either commencing from the beginning of the poem, or starting at the point where the dialogue opens. The poems, made up of short verses of (normally) four lines, have a regular structure, consisting of a brief introduction providing the setting, followed by an extended dialogue with the two protagonists speaking in alternating verses, and ending with a conclusion or doxology, usually only a single verse. There are some occasional exceptions to this pattern, as in the *sughitho* on Abraham and Isaac, based on Genesis 22: in this poem not only is there a narrative element, but also the addition of two further speakers, Sarah (who of course does not feature in the biblical narrative at all) and God.[7]

The metres employed are simple, the most frequent being 7 + 7, 7 + 7 syllables (thus the first three dialogue poems in this collection). The alphabetic acrostic in the fourth poem at first sight appears to suggest a simpler form, with just 7 + 7 syllables, but the presence of an end rhyme (-*na*) in all the even verses indicates that the verses of this poem, too, are really 7 + 7, 7 + 7, with each verse covering two letters of the alphabet. The fifth poem has verses consisting of 8 + 9 syllables, although there are several irregularities; these, however, may be due to the poorly preserved character of the text (see note 10, below). A small number of other metres are also to be found in other dialogue poems. The *sughyotho* are regularly provided with a *qolo* title, indicating the melody to which they are sung, and most will also have a Refrain (*'unoyo*). The *qolo* indicated for the first three *sughyotho* is normally given as ܀܀܀ ܀܀܀ while for the fifth it is ܀܀܀ ܀܀܀. No *qolo* title

---

[6] *Mimro* 11 of his famous *Pardayso da-'den* consists of a Dispute between the Body and the Soul.

[7] Sarah also features prominently in two Syriac narrative poems (*mimre*) on Genesis 22 (the text and translation are published in *Le Muséon* 99 (1986): 61–129); see further, Brock, S. P. "Reading between the lines: Sarah and the Sacrifice of Isaac (Gen. 22)." In Archer, L., S. Fischler and M. Wyke, eds. *Women in Ancient Societies*, 167–80. London, 1994.

is provided in the single manuscript preserving the fourth *sughitho* of this collection.

The dialogue *sughyotho* are normally transmitted in liturgical manuscripts, and many of them are connected with specific points in the liturgical year, above all the period around the Nativity and the Week of the Passion. In all of these they are to be found incorporated into the Night Office (*Lilyo*). Regrettably, over the course of time, many of the poems came to be copied only in part, sometimes with just the verses of one of the two speakers, since manuscripts were often copied for the use of only one of the two choirs (*gude*). This has meant that the *sughyotho* usually survive only in a very truncated form in more recent manuscripts of the *Fanqitho* and in printed editions; thus, for example, the Mosul edition of 1896 only has verses 6–9, 11–15, 51–52 of the dialogue between Mary and the Angel (II, pp. 94–5); although the Pampakuda edition of 1962 (I, pp. 57–9) offers rather more, only the odd-numbered verses are given, thus denying Mary any right of reply to the Angel![8] Accordingly, it is usually necessary to go back, wherever possible, to the earliest manuscripts, dating from the ninth to eleventh centuries, in order to recover the complete form of these poems;[9] in some cases the full text can only be reconstructed on the basis of a number of different manuscripts, none of which provides the poem complete.[10]

*

The dialogue poems offer a splendid combination of liveliness, psychological insight, and sound teaching, along with some gentle humour. It is a matter of regret that they have remained neglected for so long, seeing that they have a great potential for religious education, especially with children (but by no means confined to them). In recent years, however, there are a few signs emerging of their revival for use as a catechetical resource:[11] thus, for example, several have recently been translated into Arabic for catechet-

---

[8] It should be mentioned, however, that the printed edition of the Maronite *Fanqitho*, published in Rome in 1656, *does* provide the complete text (pp. 195–201).

[9] This applies to I–III of the present collection; details can be found in Brock 1984. IV is based on a single late manuscript (published in *Parole de l'Orient*: see Appendix).

[10] This applies to V, whose text (published here for the first time) is reconstructed on the basis of four different manuscripts.

[11] For this aspect, see further my "Syriac liturgical poetry: a resource for today." *The Harp. A Journal of Syriac and Oriental Studies* (Kottayam: S.E.E.R.I) 8/9 (1995/6): 53–66.

ical purposes in Amman. It is to be hoped that the present small collection, by making available translations based on the full Syriac texts, will encourage this sort of use, whether by employing the translations in their present form, or by adapting them in one way or another.

Syriac Introduction

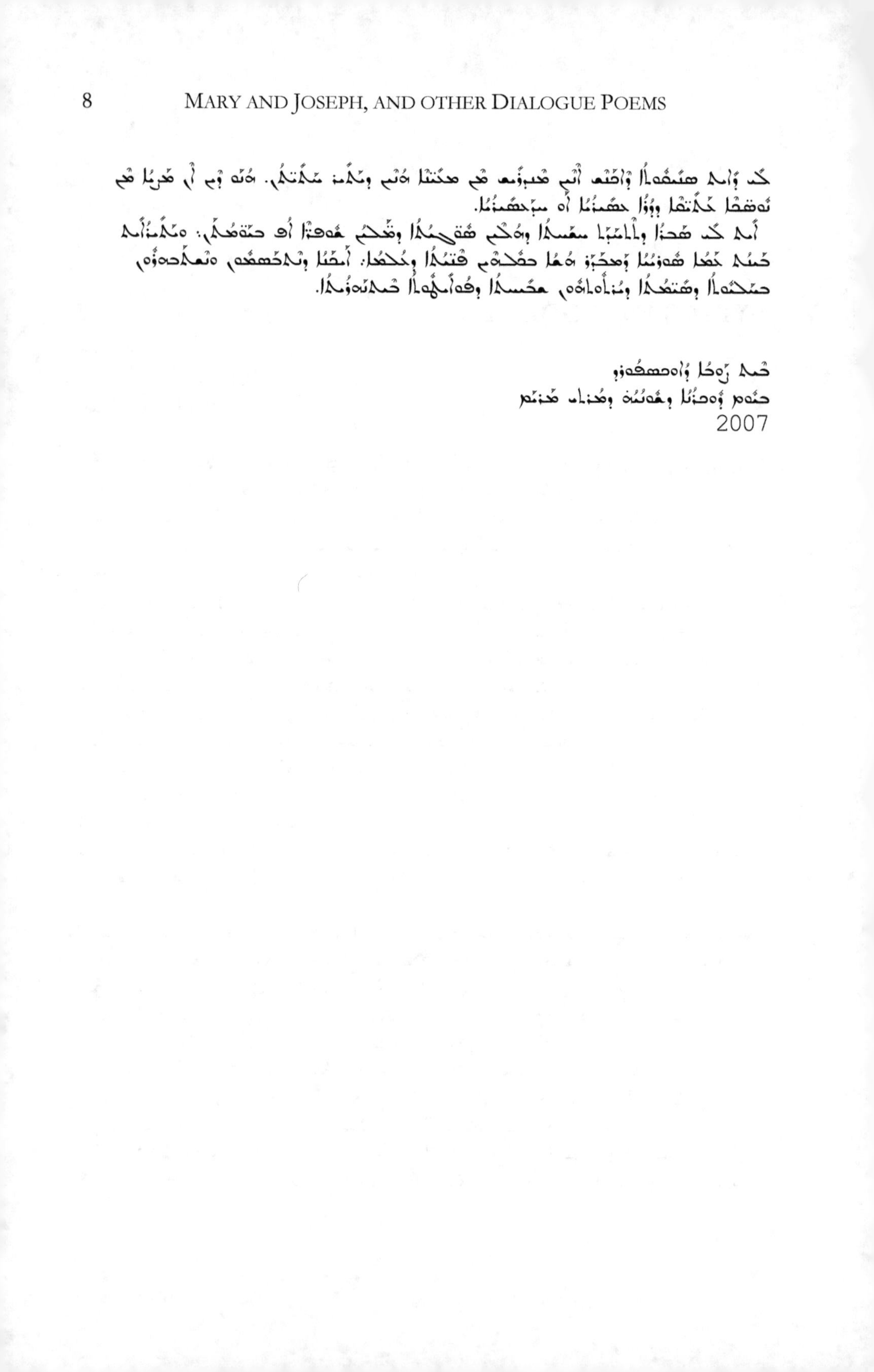

2007

TEXTS AND TRANSLATIONS

In the translations which follow an asterisk (*) draws attention to the availability of a note, to be found in the Annotation following the translations.

I. MARY AND THE ANGEL

The starting point is the Annunciation narrative in St Luke's Gospel (Luke 1:26–39), where Mary questions the angel Gabriel (Luke 1:34). In the course of the poem her 'wise questioning' is contrasted with Eve's failure to question the Serpent in Genesis. Significantly, it is only when the angel makes mention of the Holy Spirit that Mary finally accepts his message (Luke 1:38).

Refrain: Praise to You, O Lord,
     whom heaven and earth worship as they rejoice.

1. O Power* of the Father who came down and resided*,
   compelled by His love*, in a virgin womb,
   grant me utterance that I may speak
   of this great deed of Yours which cannot be grasped.

2. O Son of the Bounteous One*, whose love so willed
   that He resided in a poor girl's* womb,
   grant me utterance and words
   that in due wonder I may speak of You.

3. To speak of You the mouth is too small,
   to describe You the tongue is quite inadequate;
   voice and words are too feeble
   to relate Your beauty, so please bid me tell of You!

4. Grant that I may approach, O Lord of all*,
   in awe to that exalted place
   of the chief of the watchers* when he announced
   to the young mother Your coming.

5. You who are discerning, come, listen and give ear
   to this episode so filled with wonder;
   sing glory to Him who bent down*
   to give life to Adam who had sinned and so died.

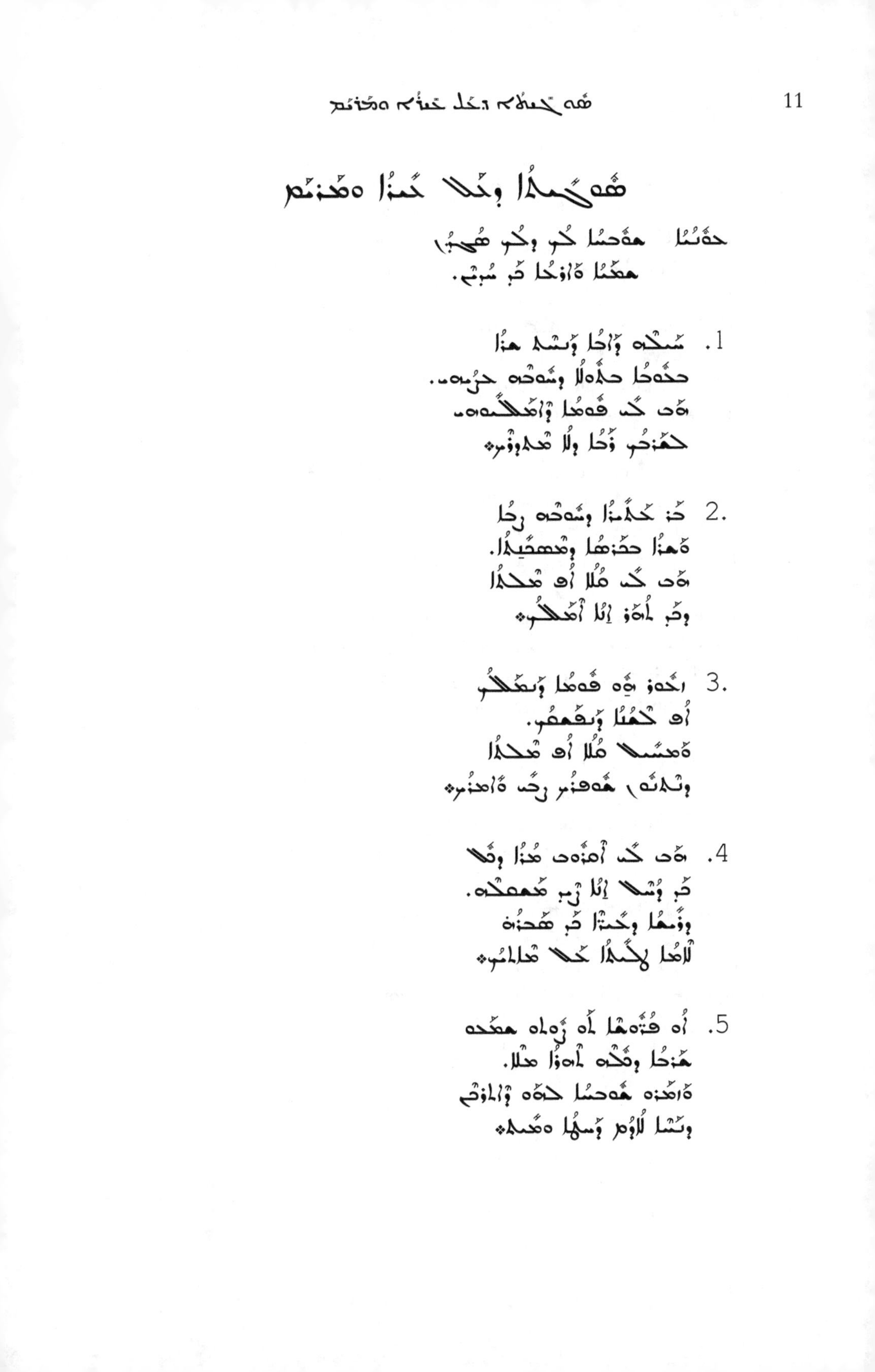

6. The Father in His mercy beckoned to His Son
   to go down and deliver what He had fashioned,
   and to Gabriel the angel He gave instructions
   to prepare the path before His descent.

7. With David's daughter* did Mercy shine out,
   for she was to be mother of Him
   who had given birth to Adam and to the world,
   and whose name is older than the sun.

8. That Will which cannot be reached flew down*
   to summon the angel, sending him out
   from the angelic ranks on his mission
   to bring glad tidings to a pure virgin.

9. He brought a letter* that had been sealed
   with the mystery that was hidden from all ages;
   he filled it with greeting to the young girl,
   and fair hope* for all the worlds.

10. The fiery being flew down until he reached
    the destitute girl*, to fill her with wealth;
    he gave her a greeting, announcing to her too
    concerning her conception, the cause of wonder to all.

11. ANGEL: To the Virgin the watcher says:
    'Peace be with you, O mother of my Lord,   Luke 1:28
    blessed are you, young woman,
    and blessed the Fruit* that is within you'.   Luke 1:42

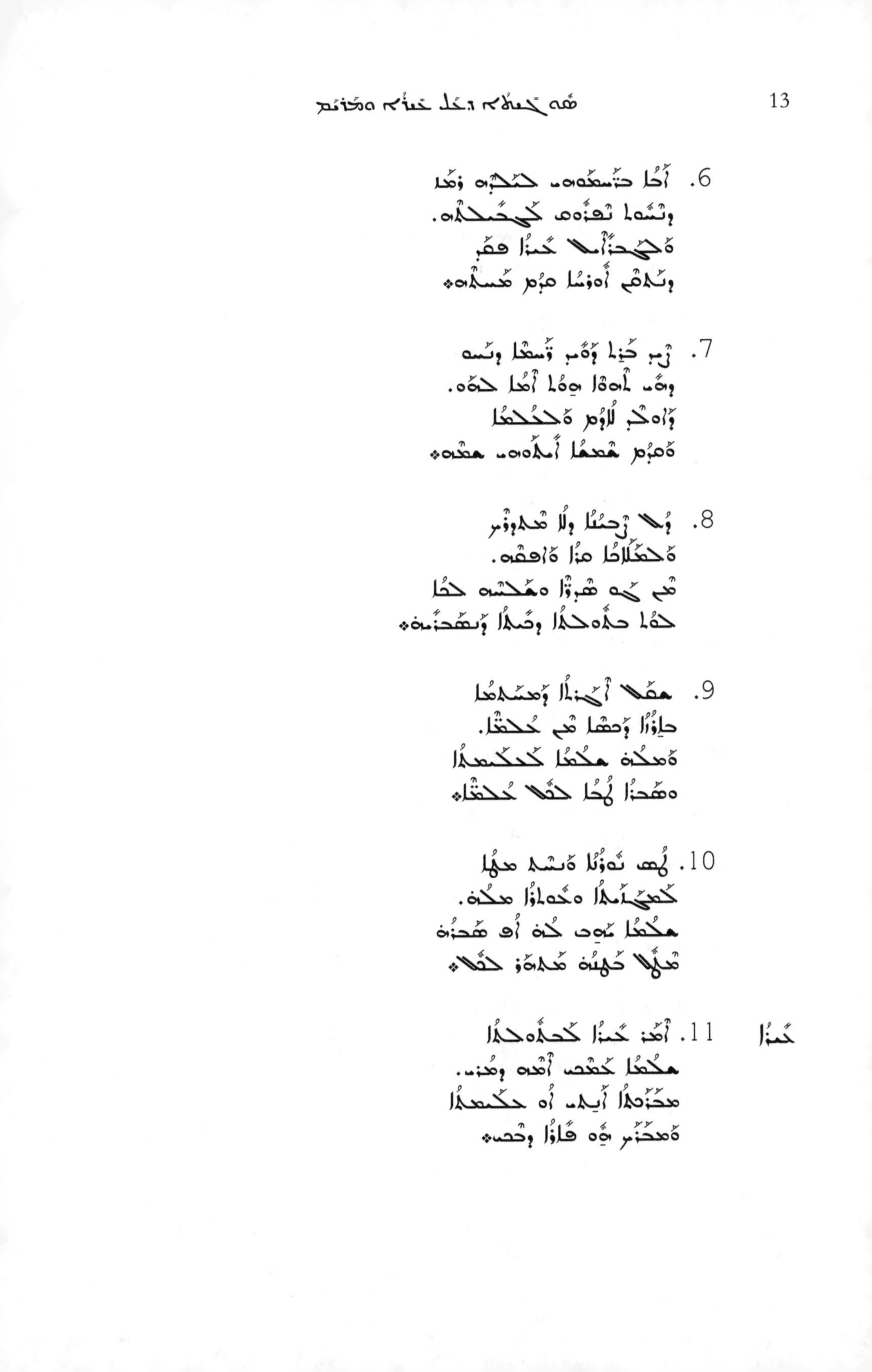

12. MARY: Says Mary, 'Who are you, sir?
And what is this that you utter?
What you are saying is remote from me,
and what it means, I have no idea'.

13. ANGEL: O blessed of women, in you has it pleased
the Most High to reside; have no fear,
for in you has Grace bent down
to pour mercy upon the world.

14. MARY: I beg you, sir, do not upset me;
you are clothed with coals of fire: mind you don't burn me.
What you are saying is alien to me
and I am unable to grasp what it means.

15. ANGEL: The Father has revealed to me, as I do so now to you,
this mystery which is shared
between Him and His Son, when He sent me to say
that from you will He shine out over the worlds.

16. MARY: You are made of flame, do not frighten me;
you are wrapped in coals of fire, do not terrify me.
O fiery being, why should I believe you
seeing that all you have spoken to me is utterly new?

17. ANGEL: It would be amazing in you if you were to answer back,
annulling the message which I have brought to you
concerning the conception of the Most High,
whose will it is to reside in your womb.

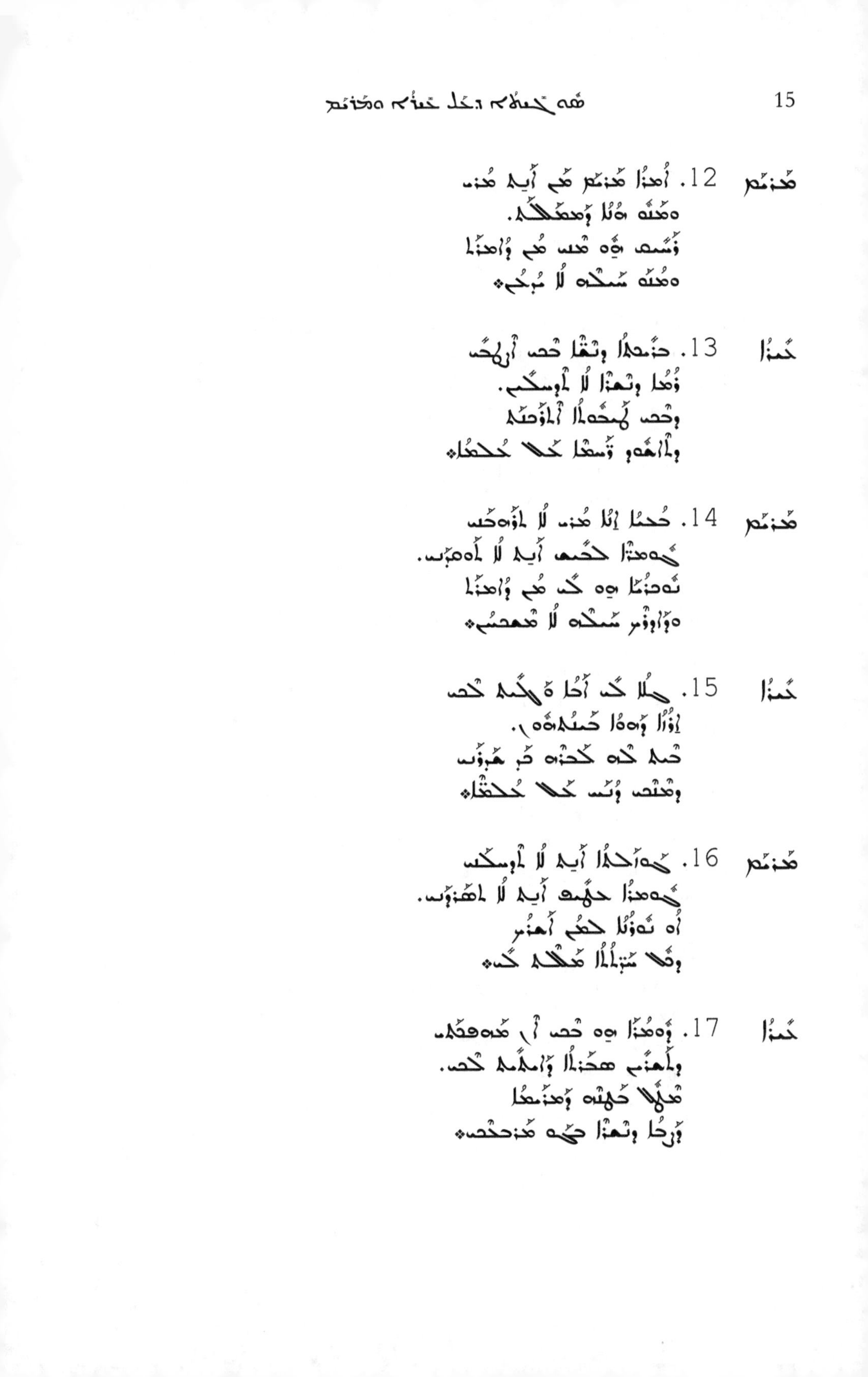

18. MARY: I am afraid, sir, to accept you,
    for when Eve my mother accepted
    the serpent who spoke as a friend,
    she was snatched away from her former glory*. Gen 3:1–7

19. ANGEL: My daughter, he certainly did use deception
    on your mother Eve when he gave her the message,
    but just as certainly I am not deceiving you now,
    since it is from the True One that I have been sent.

20. MARY: All this that you have spoken
    is most difficult, so do not find fault with me,
    for it is not from a virgin that a son will appear,
    nor from that fruit, a divine being!*

21. ANGEL: The Father gave me this meeting with you here
    to bring you greeting and to announce to you
    that from your womb His Son will shine forth.
    Do not answer back, disputing this.

22. MARY: This meeting with you and your presence here is all very well,
    if only the natural order of things did not stir me
    to have doubts at your arrival,
    for how can there be fruit in a virgin?

23. ANGEL: The angelic hosts quake at His word:
    the moment He has commanded, they do not answer back;
    how is it then that you are not afraid
    to enquire into what the Father has willed?

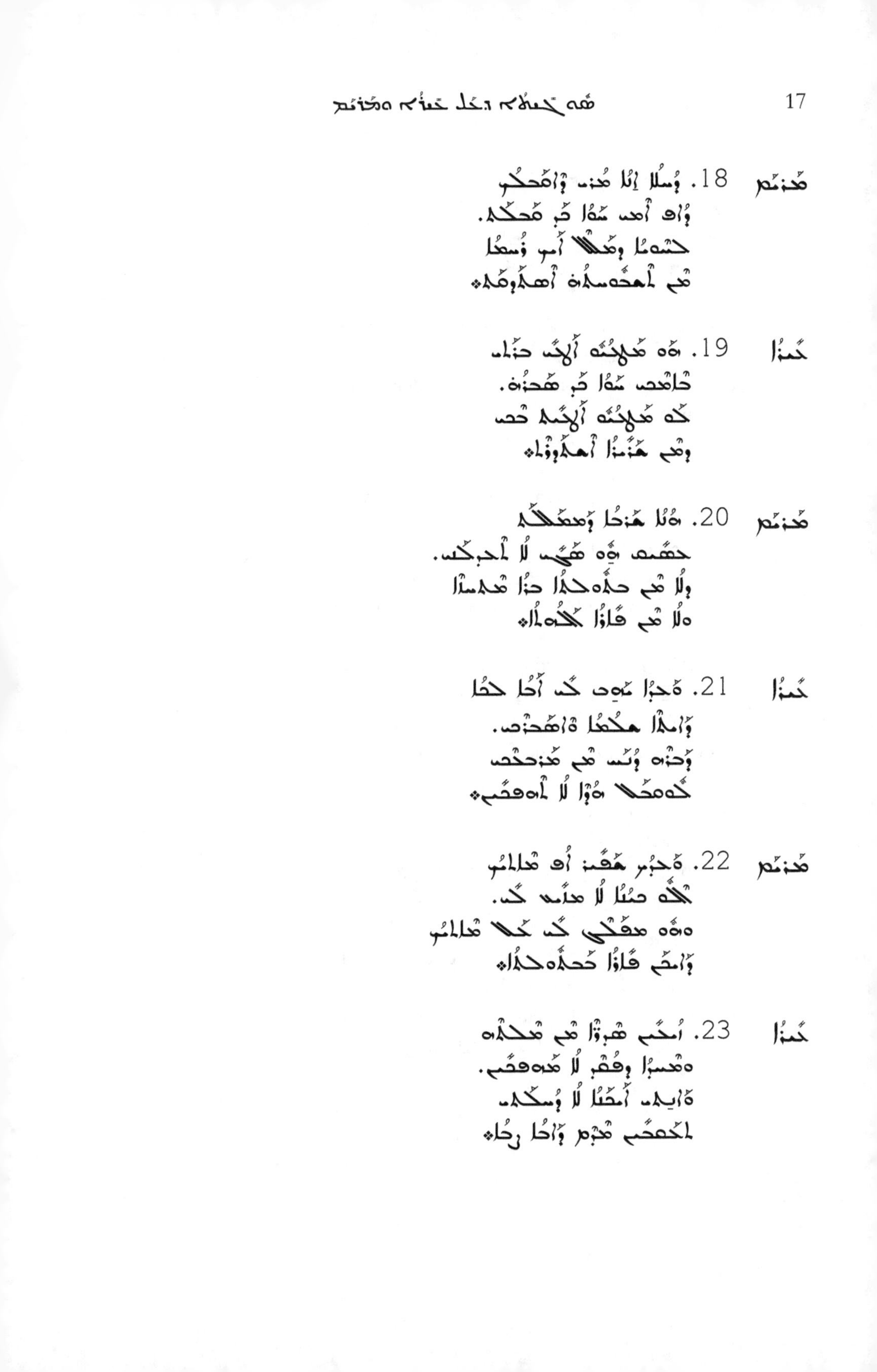

24.   MARY: I too quake, sir, and am terrified,
      yet, though I am afraid, I find it hard to believe
      since nature itself can well convince me
      that virgins do not ever give birth.

25.   ANGEL: It is the Father's love which has so willed
      that in your virginity you should give birth to the Son.
      It is appropriate you should keep silent, and have faith too,
      for the will of the Father cannot be gainsaid.

26.   MARY: Your appearance is venerable, your message full of awe,
      your flames are leaping up.
      Into the person of your Lord one cannot inquire,
      but that I should believe all this is difficult for me.

27.   ANGEL: It is glad tidings that I have brought you:
      you shall give birth to your Lord, as I have explained.
      O child, give thanks to Him who has held you worthy
      to be His mother, while having Him as your Son.

28.   MARY: I am but a girl and cannot
      receive a man of fire.
      The matter you speak of is hidden from me,
      yet you proclaim that I should accept it.

29.   ANGEL: Today for Adam hope has arrived,
      for in you is the Lord of all pleased
      to come down and release him, granting him liberty.
      Accept my words, at the same time give thanks.

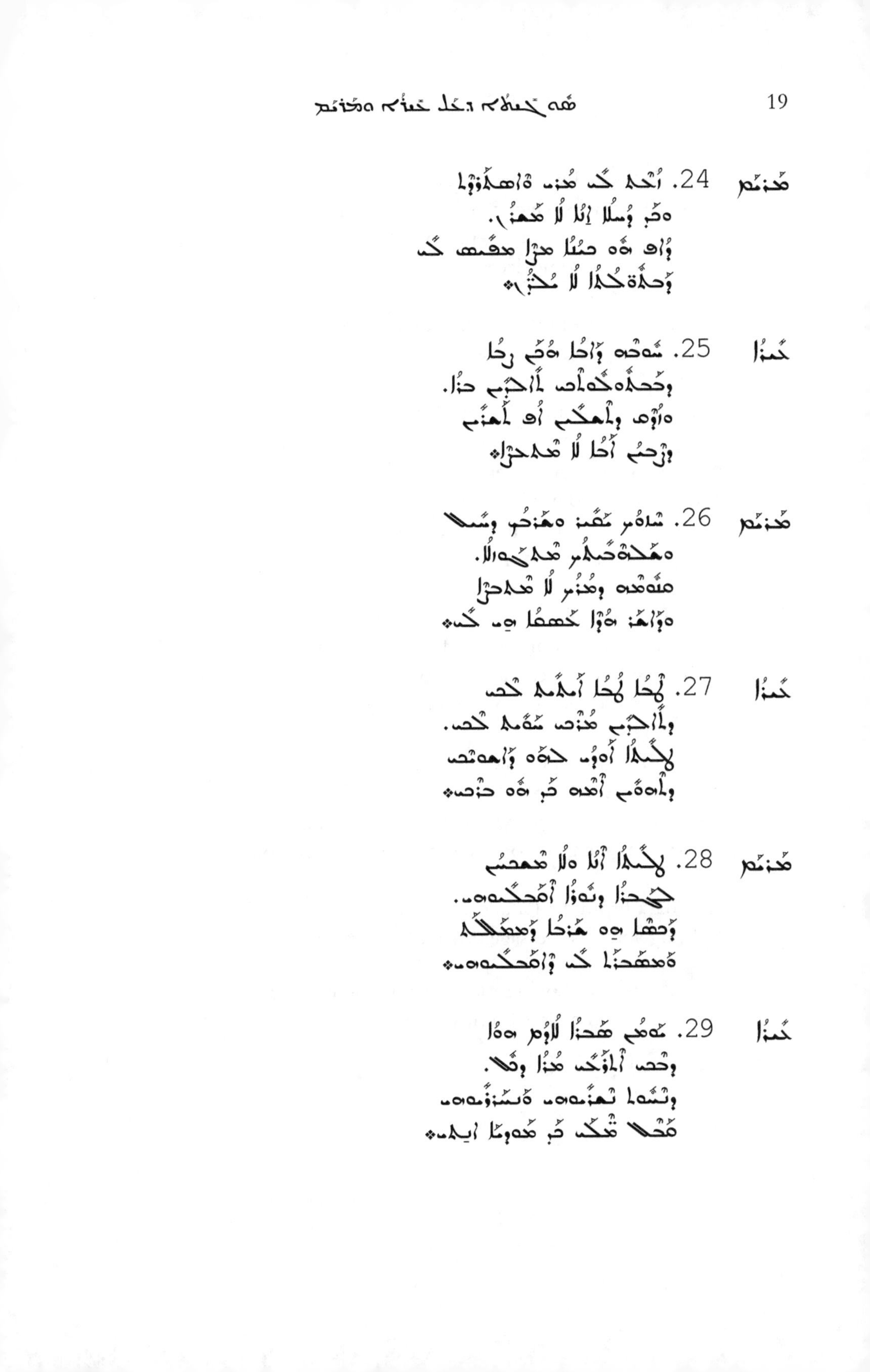

30.   MARY: Today I wonder and am amazed
      at all these things which you have said to me.
      Yet I am afraid, sir, to accept you,
      in case there is some deceit in your words.

31.   ANGEL: When I was sent to announce to you
      I heard His greeting and brought it to you.
      My Lord is true, for thus He has willed
      to shine forth from you over the worlds.

32.   MARY: All your words astonish me;
      I beg you, sir, do not blame me,
      for a son in a virgin is not to be seen,
      and no one has ever slept with me.

33.   ANGEL: He will come to you, have no fear;
      He will reside in your womb, do not ask how.
      O woman full of blessings, sing praise
      to Him who is pleased to be seen in you.

34.   MARY: Sir, no man has ever known me,
      nor has any ever slept with me.
      How can this be in the way that you have said,
      for without such a union there will never be any son?

35.   ANGEL: From the Father was I sent
      to bring you this message, for His love has compelled
            Him
      so that His Son should reside in your womb,
      and over you the Holy Spirit will reside*.   Luke 1:35

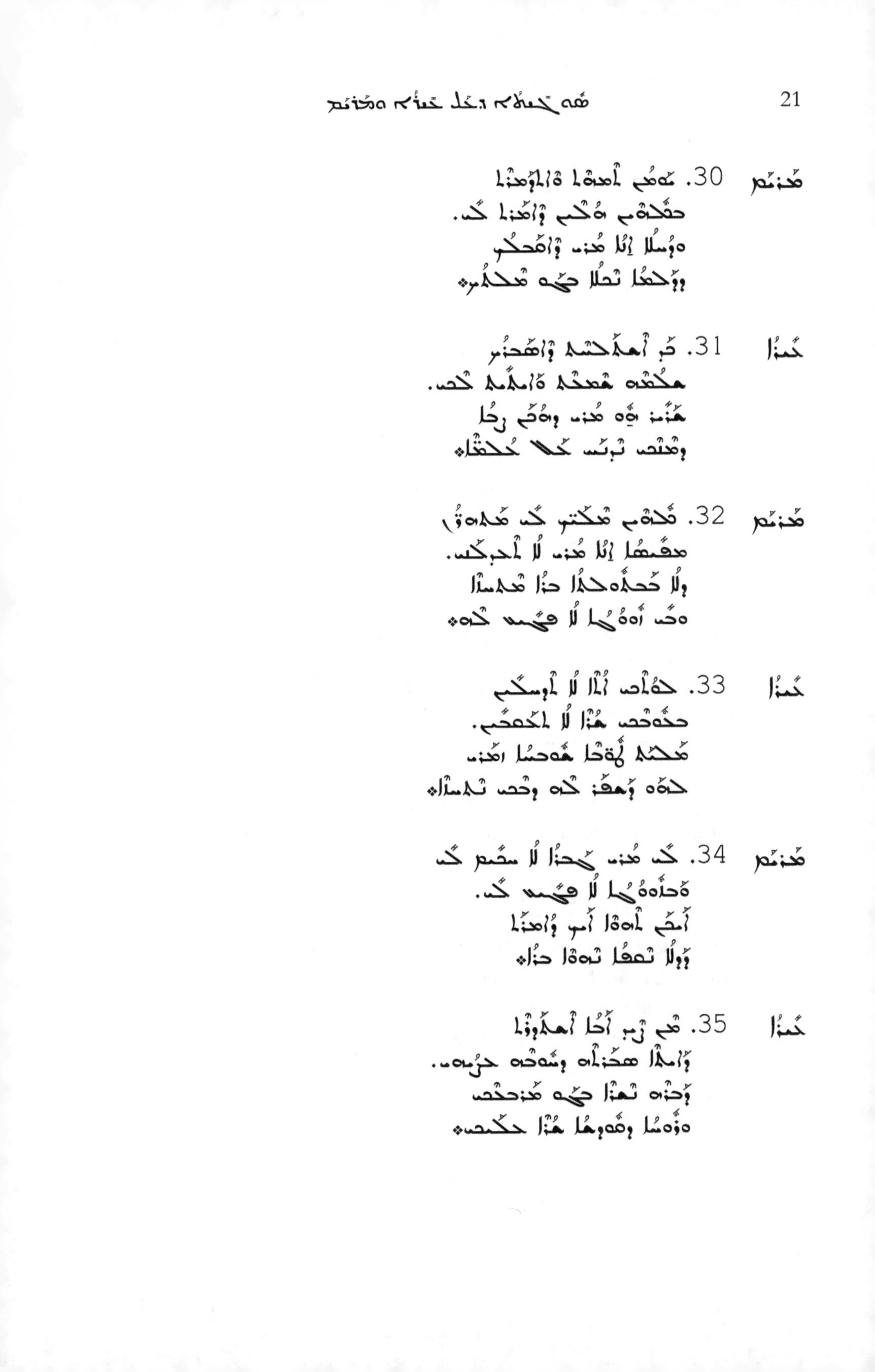

36. MARY: In that case, O watcher, I will not answer back:
    if the Holy Spirit shall come to me,
    I am His maidservant, and He has authority   Luke 1:38
    let it be to me, sir, in accordance with your word.

37. ANGEL: Let your head be raised up, O young girl,
    let your heart rejoice, O virgin;
    O Second Heaven*, let the earth   Isa 65:17
    rejoice at you, for in your Son it acquires peace.

38. MARY: Let my head be raised up, sir, as you say.
    As I rejoice, I shall confess His name,
    for if you, His servant, are so fair,
    what might He be like—if you know?

39. ANGEL: This is something the angelic hosts are unable to do,
    to gaze on Him, for He is most fearful.
    He is hidden within His Father's flame,
    and the heavenly bands quake with fear at Him.

40. MARY: You greatly disturb me now,
    for if, as you say, He is all flame,
    how will my womb not be harmed
    at the Fire residing there?

41. ANGEL: Your womb will be filled with sanctity,
    sealed with the Hidden Divinity:
    a place that is holy is greatly beloved
    by God as a place in which to appear.

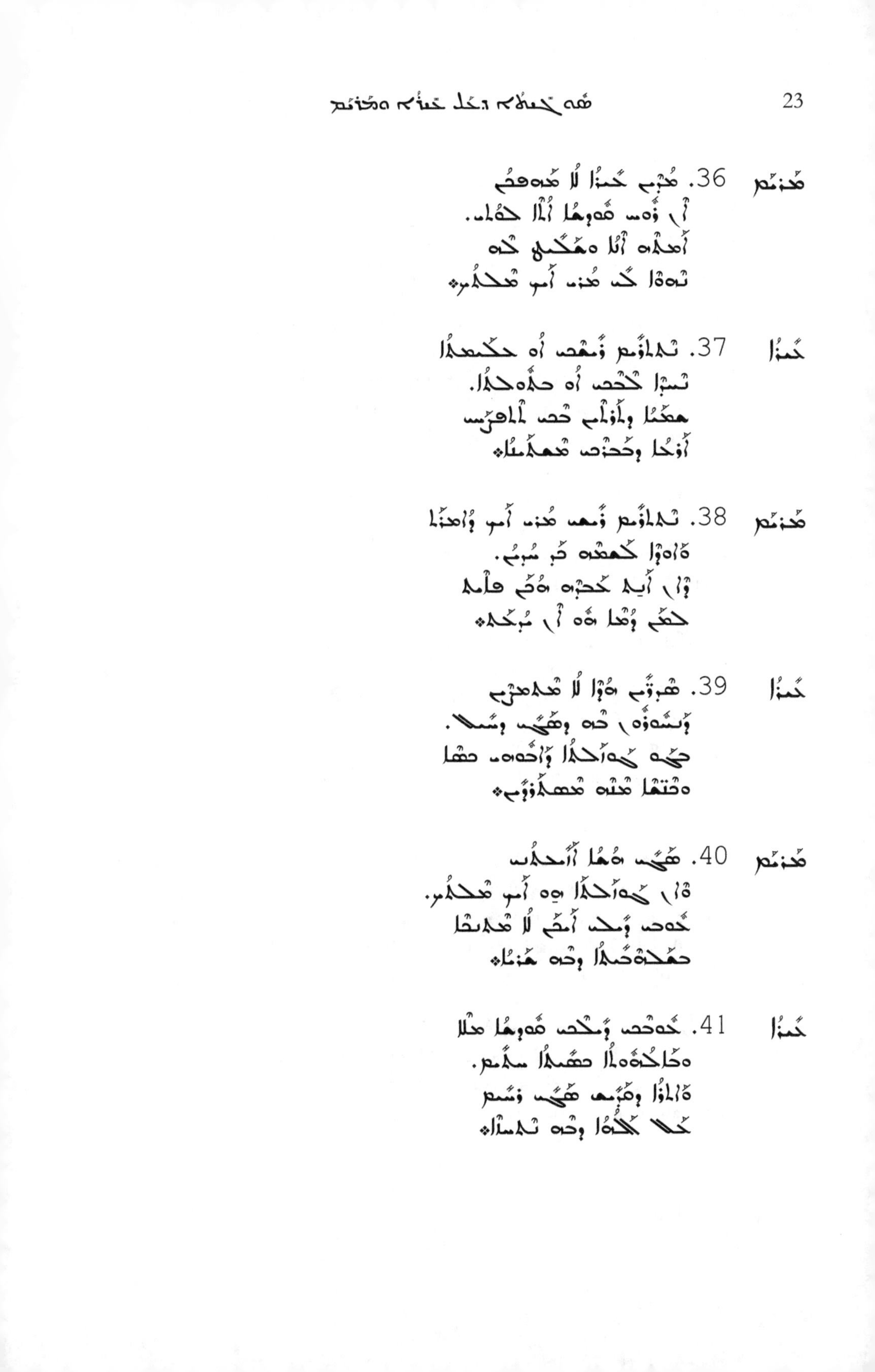

42. MARY: O watcher, reveal to me why it has pleased
your Lord to reside in a poor girl like me:
the world is full of kings' daughters,
so why does He want me who am quite destitute?

43. ANGEL: It would have been easy for Him to dwell in
a rich girl,
but it is with your poverty that He has fallen in love,
so that He may become a companion to the poor,
and enrich them once He is revealed.

44. MARY: Explain to me, sir, if you know this,
when does He wish to come to me,
and will He appear to me like fire
when He resides in me, as you have said?

45. ANGEL: He has already so willed it, He is come and
is residing within you:
it was so as not to frighten you that you remained un-
aware of Him.
I dare not look upon you
now that you are filled with the Fire that does not   cp. Exod 3:2
consume.

46. MARY: I should like, sir, to put this question to you:
explain to me the ways of my Son
who resides in me without my being aware;
what should I do for Him so that He is not held in
contempt?

47. ANGEL: Cry out 'Holy, Holy, Holy',   Isa 6:3
just as our heavenly legions do, adding nothing else,
for we have nothing besides this 'Holy';
this is all we utter concerning your Son.

مَدنِثم 42.
مَدنِثم 44.
مَدنِثم 46.

48. MARY: Holy and glorious and blessed is his name*,
    for He has looked upon His handmaid's low estate; Luke 1:48
    henceforth all generations in the world
    shall proclaim me blessed.

49. ANGEL: Height and depth shall hold Him in honour,
    angels and human kind shall give Him praise,
    for He, the Lord of all, has come down
    and resided in a virgin, so as to make all things new.

50. MARY: Great is His mercy and not to be measured,
    far beyond what lips can describe;
    on high the heavens cannot contain Him,
    yet below for Him a womb suffices!

51. Let heaven and earth call Him blessed;
    let both the angel and the Virgin,
    and all humanity too, call Him holy,
    for in His love He has descended and become a human being!

52. Let heaven and the watchers give thanks on high,
    and let earth rejoice in the Virgin;
    let both sides, as they exult,
    give praise to the Son of their Lord.

53. Let both sides be mingled in praise,
    both watchers and human beings,
    to the Son who has restored peace between them, Col 1:20–21
    when there had been anger and disruption.

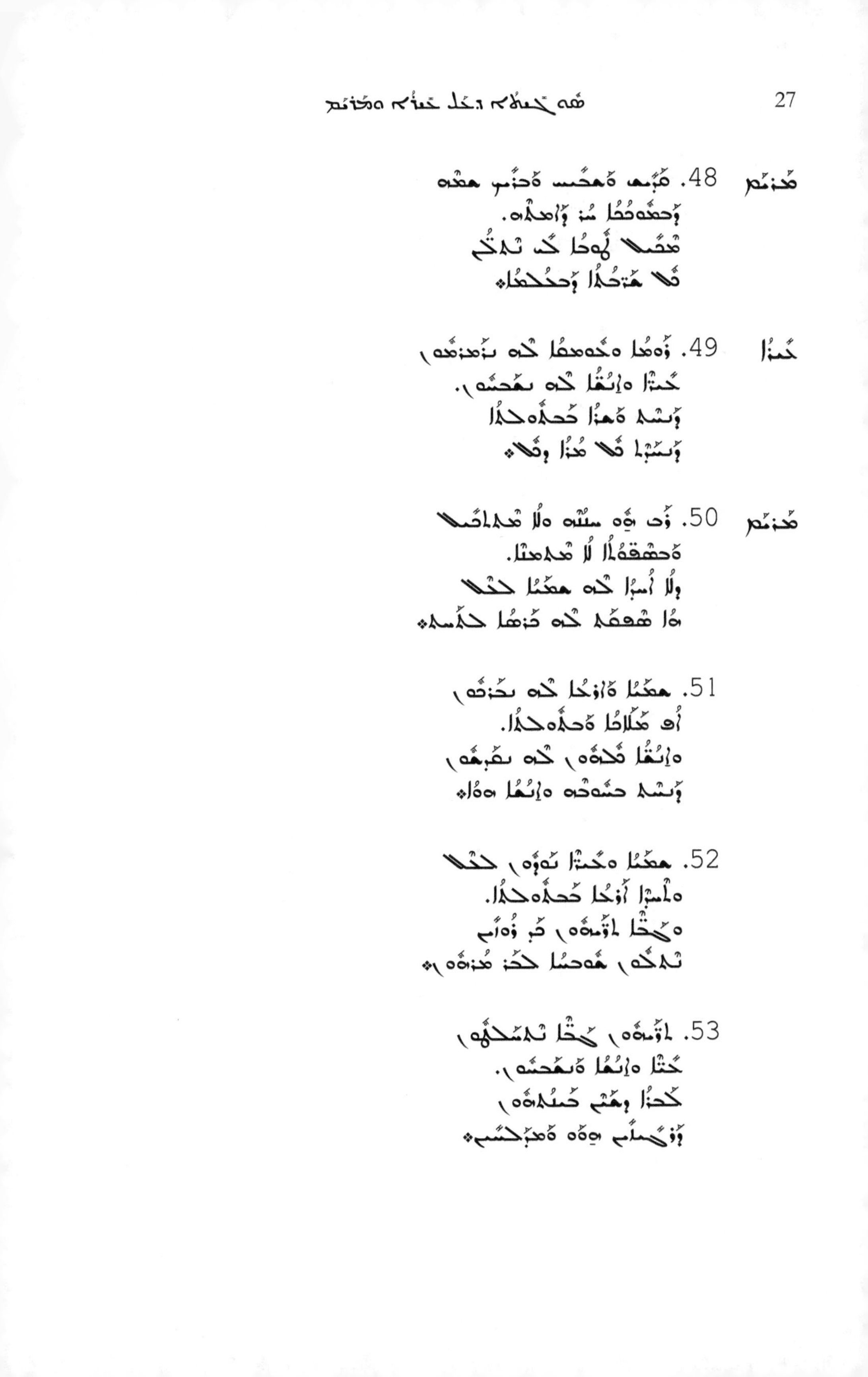

54. Thanks be to You, Lord, from all the fiery
    and invisible worlds;
    in this world, too, from every mouth
    let the earth sing praises to You.

54. ܐܘܪܚ ܟܠ ܡܕܢ ܡܢ ܩܕܡܘܗܝ
ܡܬܩܢ ܗܘܐ ܘܠܐ ܡܬܗܦܟ.
ܘܡܢ ܩܠܐ ܦܘܩܕܢܝ ܕܡܬܠܚܡܐ
ܐܪܥܐ ܐܘܪܚܐ ܟܠ ܐܡܬܝ܀

II. MARY AND JOSEPH

The poem imaginatively recreates the moment when Joseph returns home to find his fiancée pregnant by (as he naturally supposes) another man (Matthew 1:18). Reason tells Joseph that Mary's explanation of what had happened to her was impossible, and it is only Mary's perseverance which finally leads him to agreeing to divorce her quietly (Matthew 1:19). Mary then assures Joseph that the Child in her womb will himself reveal the truth of the matter, at which point he finally concedes that there might be something in what she is saying. It is only when Joseph has reached this point, where reason begins to allow that Mary's faith, as manifested by her persistence, might have a firm basis after all, that verification follows, with the angel reassuring Joseph in his sleep (Matthew 1:20).

Refrain: Praise to You, Lord, for at Your coming
   sinners turned from their wickedness
   and entered into the protection of Eden's Garden,
   which is the holy church.

1. Our Lord performed a wonder, my brethren,
   when He came down and resided in a Virgin—
   betrothed, chaste and excellent:
   her womb was sealed and her conception glorious.

2. An angel brought a greeting of peace and gave it   Luke 1:28
   to the daughter of poor parents, filling her with wealth;
   she received a conception that astonishes everyone,
   treating it with wonder.

3. In her womb was the Child who fashions all*,
   in her breasts was the milk* which astonishes all.
   Her virginity was sealed, yet her womb was full,
   she was pregnant with child, but the secret was hidden.   Matt 1:18

4. Joseph was dumfounded at Mary,
   seeing her pregnancy of which he knew nothing.
   He began to chide and reproach her,
   saying, Listen, girl;

5. JOSEPH: Reveal to me the secret of what has happened to you;
   it is greatly shocking, what you speak of:
   who has led you astray, virgin,
   and snatched away your wealth, chaste girl?

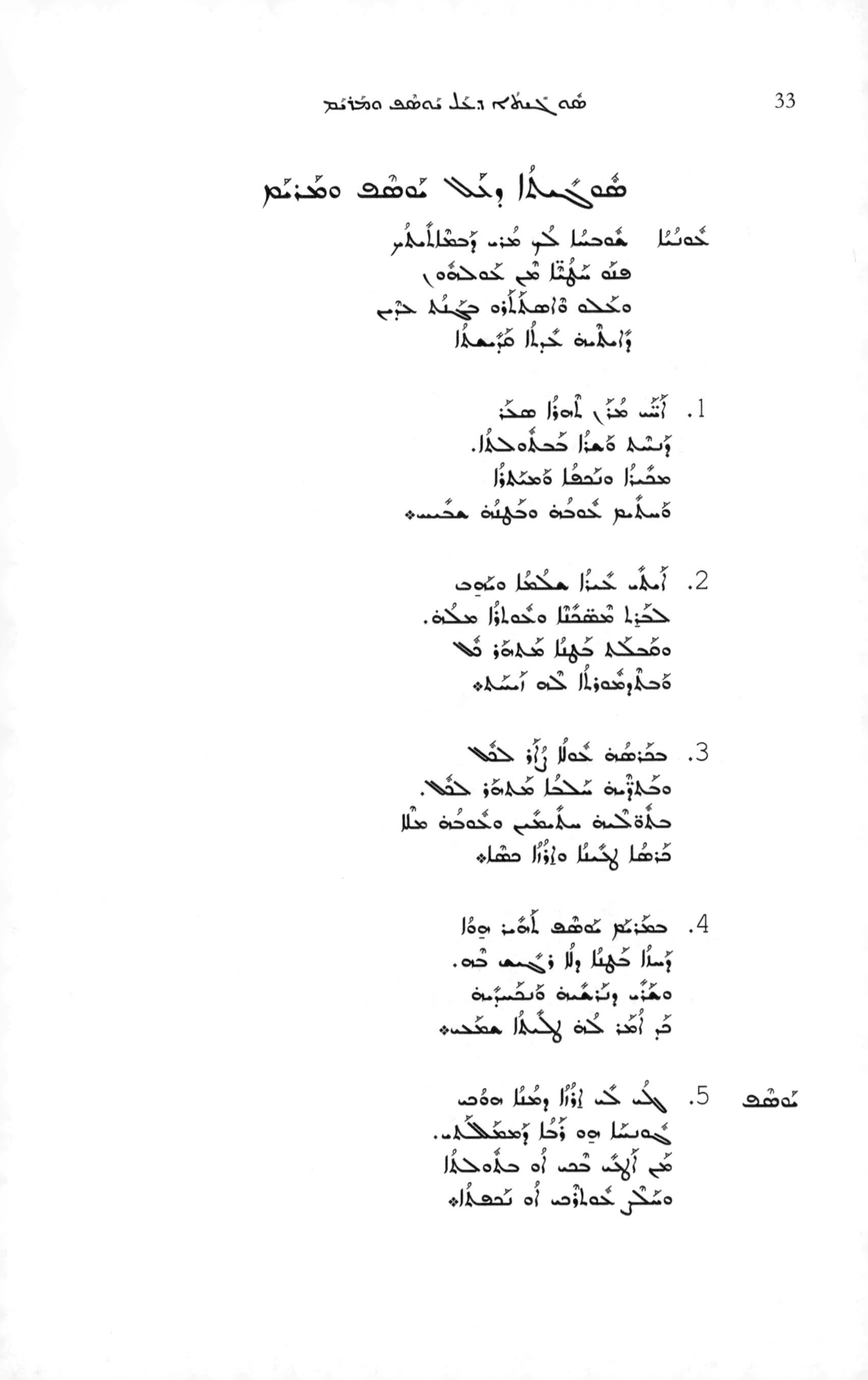

6. MARY: I will reveal to you how it happened.
   says Mary, So listen, Joseph.
   A man of fire came down to me,
   he gave me a greeting - and this took place.

7. JOSEPH: That I should believe this is hard:
   it is not good, so do not repeat it.
   If you are willing, speak to me
   about what took place: who led you astray?

8. MARY: How to tell you any more I do not know,
   for I have told you how it actually happened:
   the chief of the watchers came down and announced
       it to me;
   I became pregnant without being aware of it.

9. JOSEPH: These words are inappropriate,
   Mary, for a virgin; keep silent,
   for falsehood will not stand up.
   Speak the truth, if you are willing.

10. MARY: I repeat the very same words—
    I have no others to say.
    I remain sealed, as the seals of my virginity,
    which have not been loosed, will testify.

11. JOSEPH: You ought not to contradict,
    but confess that you have been seduced.
    Now you have fallen into two wrongs:
    after getting pregnant, you are telling lies.

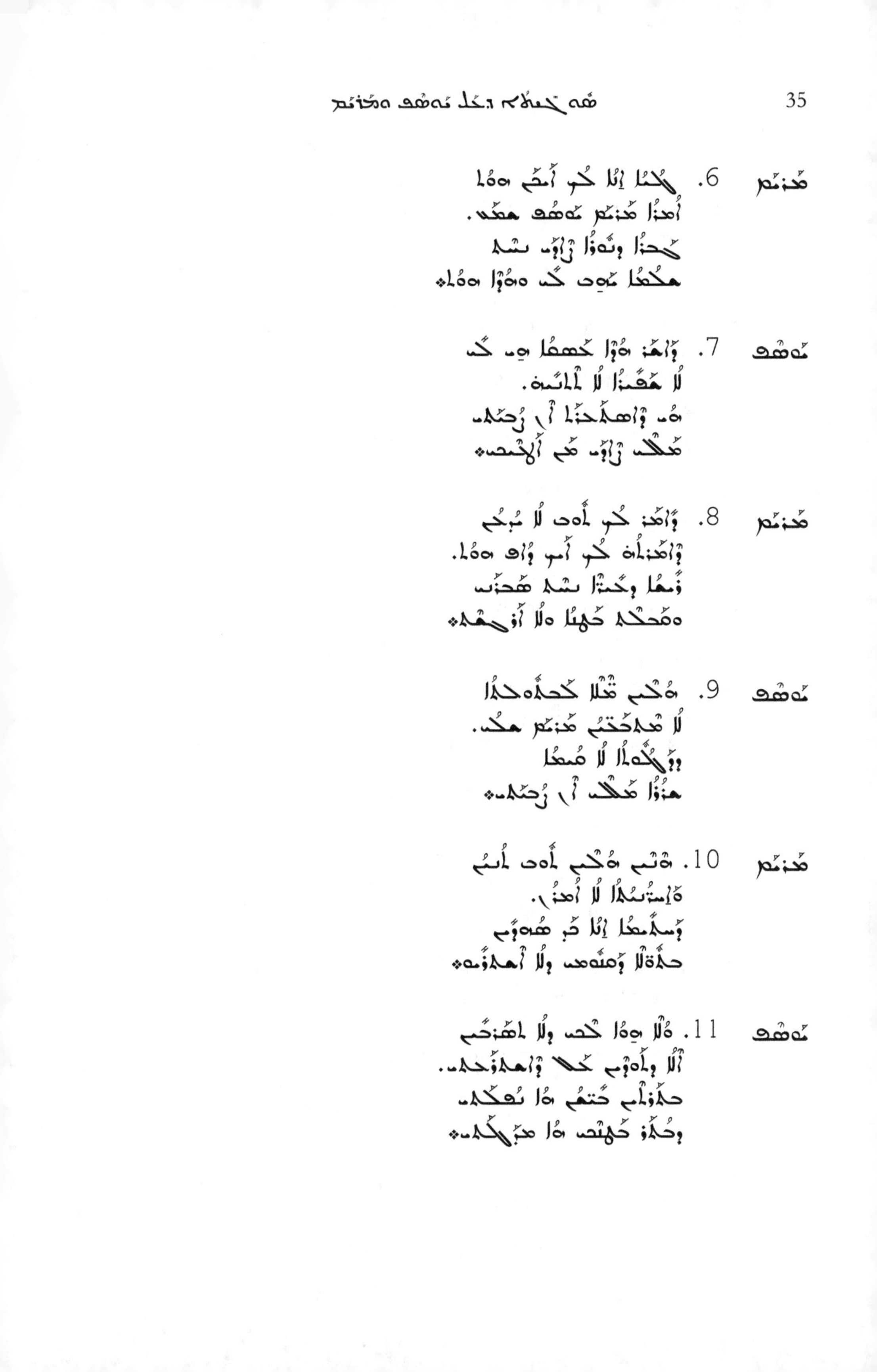

12. MARY: You ought to believe my words,
    for you have never seen any falsehood in me:
    my chaste and truthful way bear me witness
    that I am a virgin and have not lied.

13. JOSEPH: It is a cause of great fright, what you are saying:
    how can I listen to what you are saying?
    A virgin does not get pregnant
    unless she has intercourse or gets married.

14. MARY: It is a cause of great fright that you don't believe,
    for it is easy for the Lord of all
    to give fruit to a virgin—
    as happened with the lamb from the branch*.   Gen 22:13

15. JOSEPH: Eve was married to Adam,
    and from that union she had many children,   Gen 5:4
    whereas you alone brazenly assert
    that your womb is full without any man being involved.

16. MARY: Eve is actually a witness to my words,
    for she came into being without any intercourse,   Gen 2:21–2
    issuing from Adam* who produced her as fruit.
    So why do you not believe me?

17. JOSEPH: You have gone astray like water, chaste girl;
    just take the Scriptures and read
    how virgins do not conceive
    without intercourse, as you are claiming.

مدرشا 12.
مدرشا 14.
مدرشا 16.

18. MARY: You have gone astray, Joseph; take and read
       for yourself:
    in Isaiah it is written all about me,
    how a virgin shall have fruit.   Isa 7:14
    If that is not true, do not accept my word.

19. JOSEPH: It would befit you to be ashamed
    of the affair which is open to all;
    but now, after getting pregnant, you tell falsehoods,
    saying you are a virgin, to use your own words.

20. MARY: It would befit you, if only you were willing,
    to believe my words, for I am not telling lies.
    I remain sealed, as silent nature
    which has no voice testifies.

21. JOSEPH: Now you are glorying in falsehood
    which will not stand up, young girl.
    It is not possible in one and the same body
    for the seals of virginity to remain after conception.

22. MARY: Now you are causing me pain, Joseph,
    for I am pure, and there are witnesses:
    summon the local midwives*
    and see how my seals of virginity have not been
       loosed.

23. JOSEPH: Do you know of anyone else like you,
    who resembles you, according to what you claim?
    To you alone has this happened—
    because it simply is not true.

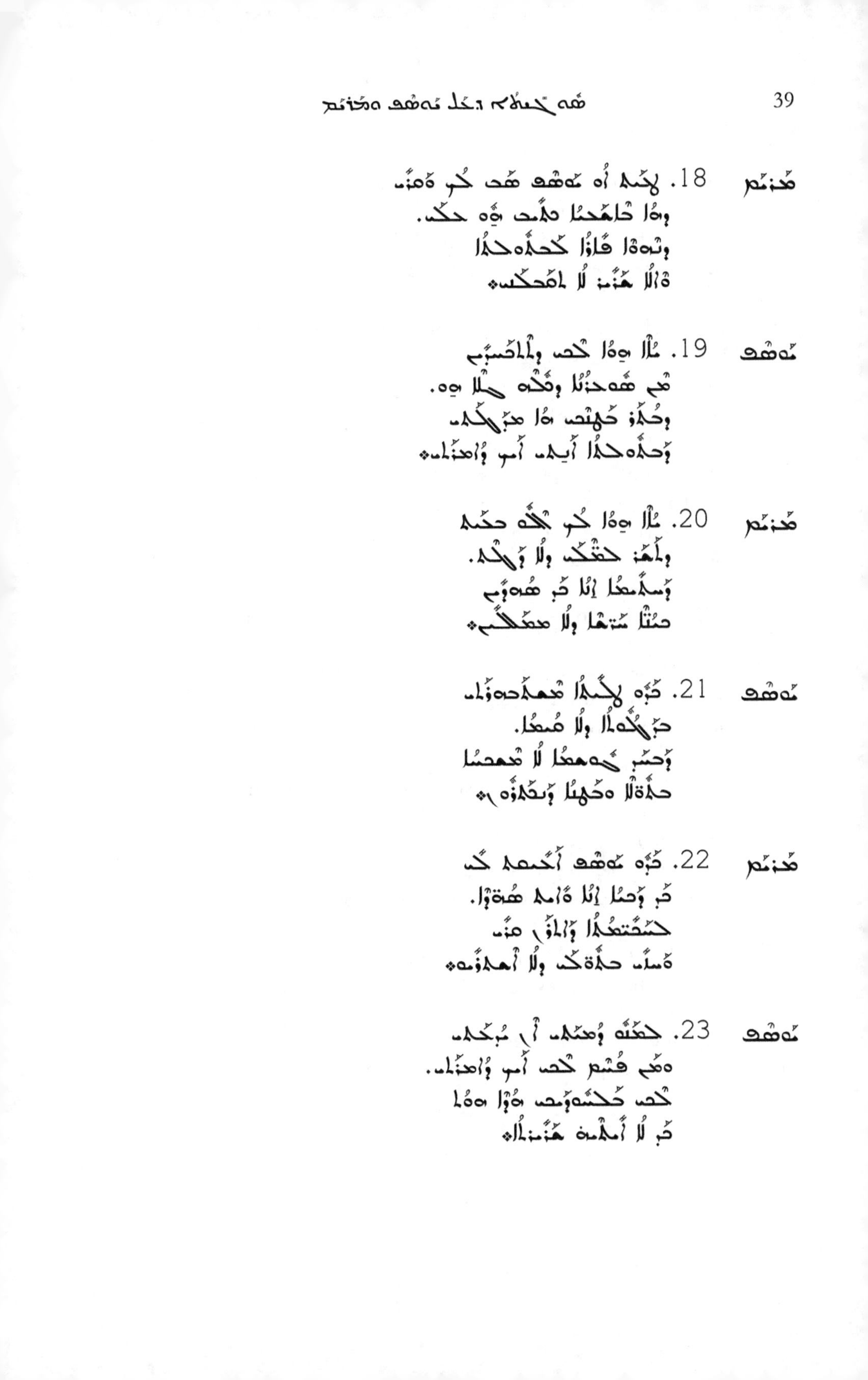

24. MARY: I do not have to be like anyone else,
    for my Son has no fellow companion:
    He is unique, and it is not possible
    for another conception like mine to take place.

25. JOSEPH: So then something quite new in the world
    has started with you, or so you claim?
    You have no proof at all,
    and there is no explanation to what you say.

26. MARY: I have no fear of any 'explanation':
    you have one to see, if only you would look.
    Who caused the stone on Horeb to flow with water,   Exod 17:6
    or who made that staff sprout forth fruit?   Num 17:8

27. JOSEPH: Let your mouth be silent, for your womb is full:
    it stands as your accuser, yet you have no fear!
    The very facts testify against you,
    and you will not even keep silent.

28. MARY: Let your mouth be silent and not pour blame on me,
    for I am not to be blamed in the eyes of anyone else:
    I am betrothed to you, as you are well aware.
    Do not let your idea of truth accuse me, Joseph.

29. JOSEPH: It is very hard for me to believe you,
    that you have not exchanged me for another, as you are saying,
    for I know that I have no part in your conception;
    so it is quite apparent that you are telling lies.

ܡܪܝܡ   24. ܠܐ ܐܢܘܢ ܗܘܘ ܐܘܠܕܐ ܠܐܠܗܐ
ܘܠܐ ܗܘܐ ܐܝܟ ܟܠܗ ܡܚܕܐ ܠܚܕܐ.
ܦܣܝܩܐܝܬ ܗܘ ܘܠܐ ܡܬܚܫܒܐ
ܘܟܗܝܢܐ ܐܝܬܘܗܝ ܐܝܟ ܕܝܟ ܕܗܘܐ܀

ܝܘܣܦ   25. ܚܠܦܝܟ ܡܪܬܝ ܗܐ ܡܪܝܡ
ܣܒܪܐ ܕܟܠܟܗܘܢ ܐܝܟ ܕܐܡܪܬܝ.
ܘܠܐ ܐܣܬܟܠܬ ܚܕܐ ܠܐ ܐܝܟ ܚܕܐ
ܘܠܐ ܦܘܡܩܐ ܚܦܝ ܕܐܡܪܬܝ܀

ܡܪܝܡ   26. ܡܢ ܦܘܡܩܐ ܠܐ ܢܦܩ
ܕܐܝܟ ܕܝ ܕܐܡܪܐ ܐܢ ܫܢܝܐ.
ܚܛܦܐ ܚܫܘܒܬ ܡܢ ܐܢܘܢܗ
ܘܕܗܒܐ ܣܒܪܐ ܡܢ ܐܢܘܢܗ܀

ܝܘܣܦ   27. ܢܗܠܐ ܦܘܡܟܝ ܘܟܘܕܟܝ ܡܠܐ
ܘܡܩܪܒܢܝ ܠܚܕܐ ܘܠܐ ܢܦܟܐܢ.
ܗܘ ܦܘܡܚܕܢܐ ܗܘܗܝ ܚܟܡܬ
ܘܐܦܠܐ ܕܐܡܟܝ ܠܐ ܙܕܩܐܢ܀

ܡܪܝܡ   28. ܢܗܠܐ ܦܘܡܢܝ ܘܠܐ ܢܟܣܢܐ
ܘܠܐ ܚܣܝܢܕܐ ܐܢܐ ܟܐܩܦܐ ܐܣܢܝ.
ܘܕܝ ܐܠܗܕܢܐ ܗܐܝܟ ܢܪܟܕ
ܡܬܘܠܝ ܝܘܣܦ ܠܐ ܬܚܡܩܢܣ܀

ܝܘܣܦ   29. ܗܝܟ ܟܣܡܐ ܕܐܘܡܥܢܬ
ܘܠܐ ܣܟܠܩܡܢܣ ܐܝܟ ܕܐܡܪܬܝ.
ܕܐܢܐ ܚܟܝܢܬ ܠܐ ܕܟܢܣ ܐܢܐ
ܘܐܬܒܪܟܕ ܟܕ ܘܐܢܐ ܐܟܕܐܢ܀

30. MARY: It is very easy for you to believe me:
my Son has one of the watchers
of fire and spirit who will testify in a revelation
whether or not I am false.

31. JOSEPH: An action cannot be done away with by words—
and your words are opaque, while your womb is full:
the very facts testify against you;
your telling lies is quite unnecessary.

32. MARY: The cause of it is too hard for you or me to grasp,
but it compels me and so I speak.
As long as my truthfulness is not impugned
I will not bow my head or feel ashamed.

33. JOSEPH: There is error in your words, virgin,
so that one is afraid for you after what you have said.
Take the bill of divorce peacefully, and be off: Matt 1:19
for my part, the secret will not be revealed.

34. MARY: It is easy for the Child who resides in my womb
to speak on my behalf when I am overcome;
He will reveal the mystery that has happened to me,
He will explain to you that I have not been false.

35. JOSEPH: Listen to what I shall say to you, O wise woman:
though I will believe what you say,
I do not dare to approach
your pure womb, for it is filled with fire.

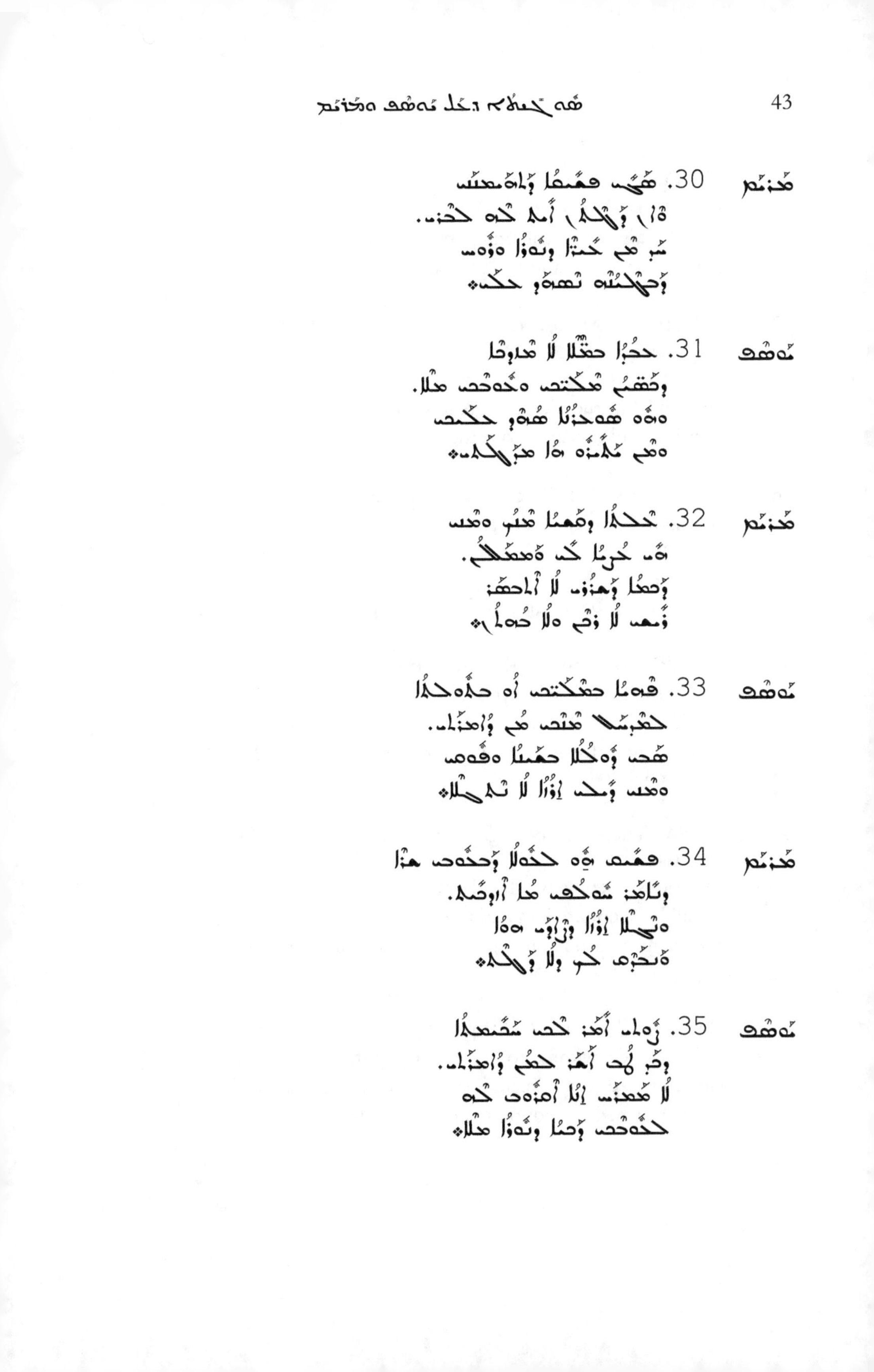

36. MARY: Your utterance is dear to me, Joseph.
    I have no desire for intercourse:
    the Child in my womb will persuade you
    that I am a virgin and have not played false.

37. JOSEPH: There are two possibilities, and both disturb me:
    if it is true, it is most frightening for me,
    but if it is untrue, that is a great grief.
    I wish I could escape from the two.

38. MARY: Now I shall pour out my words
    and address my Son hidden in my womb;
    He will reveal to you that I shall have no other children,
    and shall not be deprived of your company.

39. JOSEPH: Weighty is the matter you speak of,
    and I am afraid at what you say.
    All the more do I want
    to run away from you; why do you make me distraught?

40. MARY: There will be a great commotion concerning me,
    and foolish people will hassle me;
    I shall be accounted an adulteress,
    and if my Son does not look after me I shall be torn to pieces*.

41. Mary's Lord saw her truthfulness,
    and became a witness to her in her plight;
    He motioned to a ministering angel who came down
    and confirmed the young woman's words.

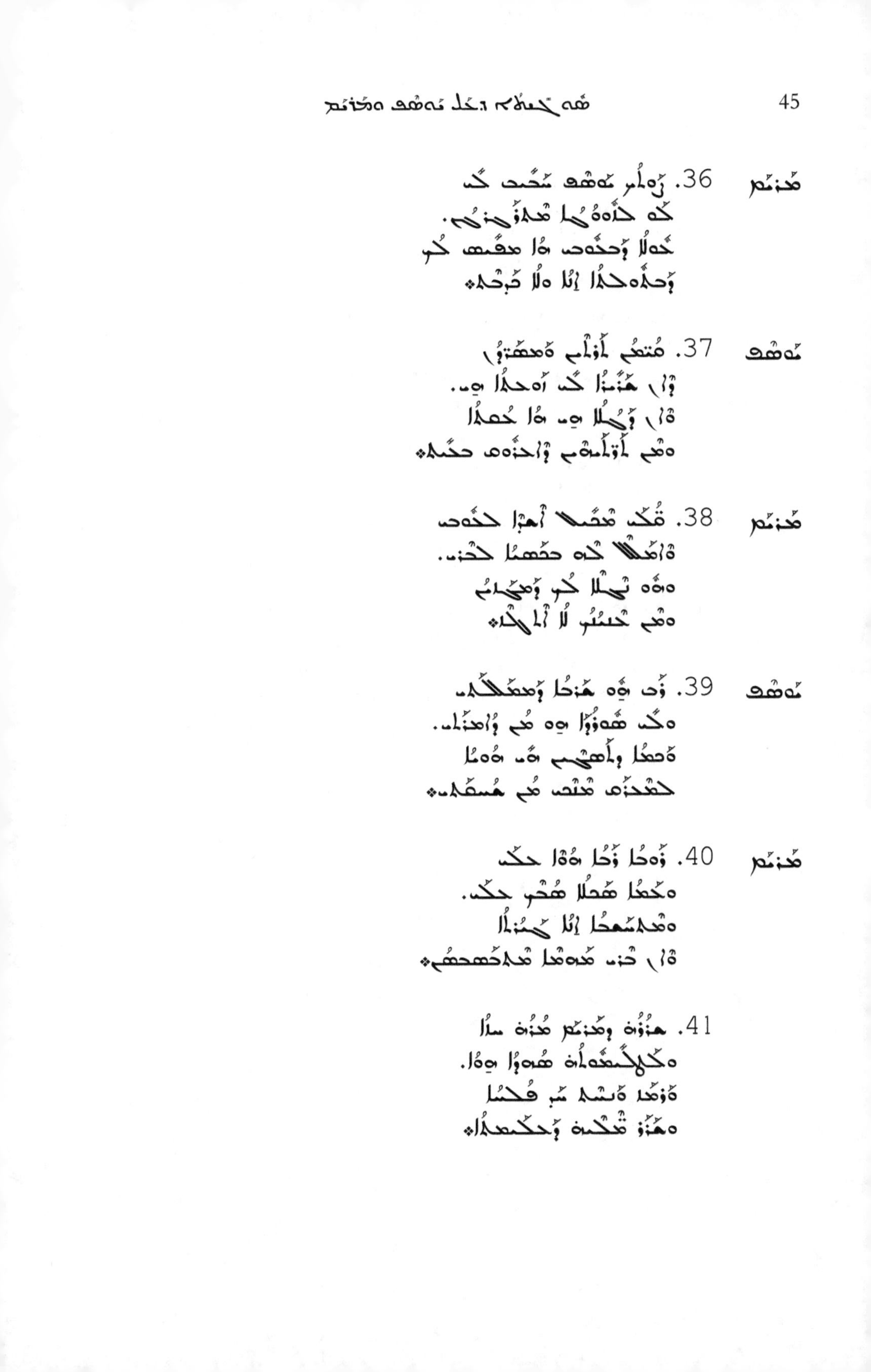

42. Joseph slept, and the watcher arrived,   Matt 1:20
    revealing to him how the mystery had taken place.
    Joseph rose up early and knelt in worship   Matt 1:24
    before Mary, full of wonder, who had not lied.

43. The upright man in wonder at the young woman,
    honoured the virgin greatly.
    Thanks be to the Son who shone forth from her,
    who delivered both worlds at His birth.

44. 'Thanksgiving be to the Lord of all',
    said Joseph to the Virgin,
    'for He so willed it and has resided in your womb
    so as to give life to all at His nativity'.

45. Thanksgiving be to Him, and blessed be the name
    of the Word who resided in the Virgin,
    remaining nine months in her womb,
    so as to save Adam. To Him be all praises!

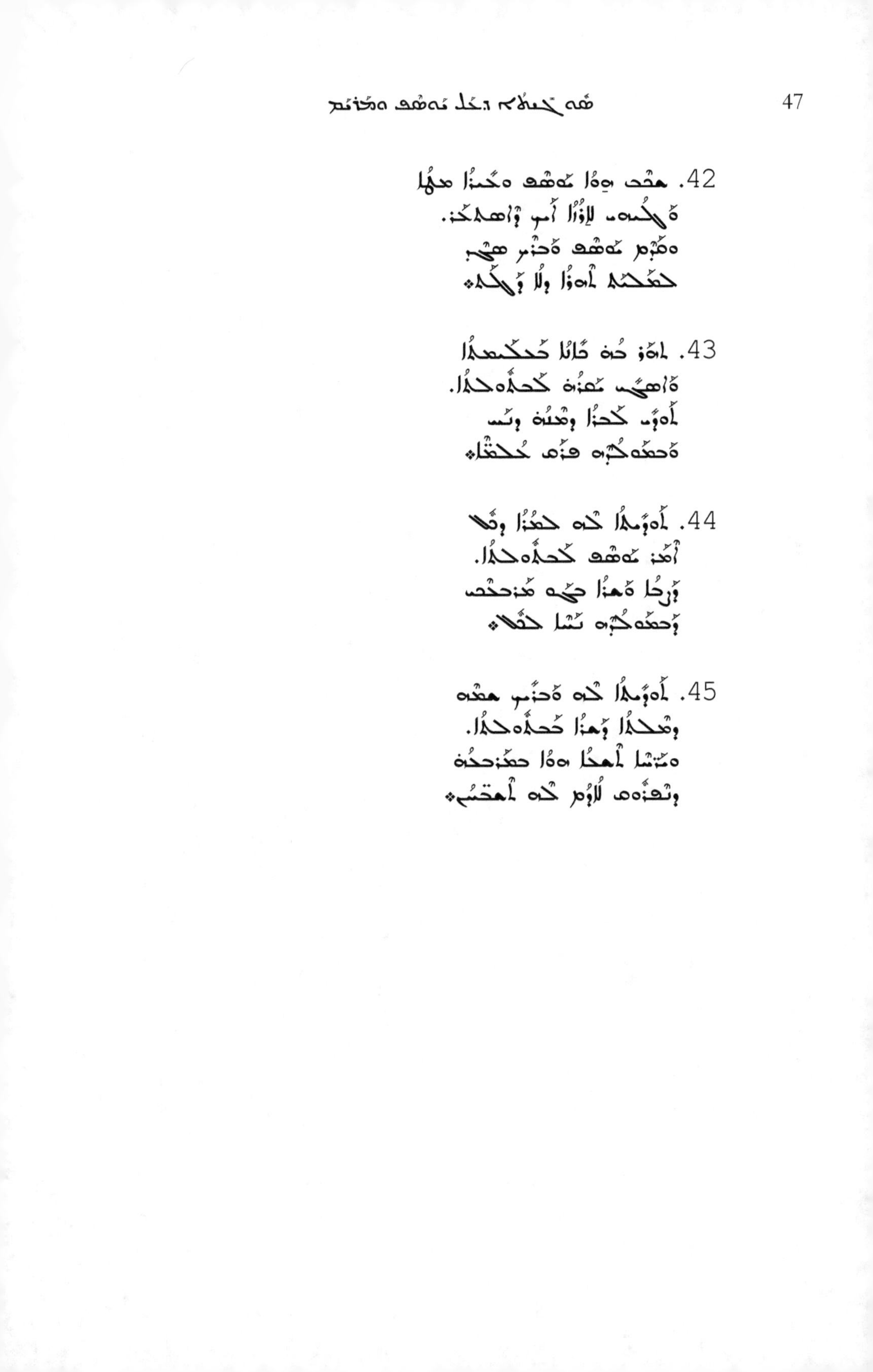

III. Mary and the Magi

When the Magi turn up with their expensive presents (Matthew 2:11) Mary at first cross-questions them, suggesting that they might have come to the wrong place. It is only when they persist in assuring her that they have not made a mistake that Mary gives a hint that she is really well aware of why they have come, but she is afraid that Herod, on learning of it all, will shed innocent blood (Matthew 2:16). Eventually, near the end of the poem Mary reveals to the Magi the message which the angel Gabriel had brought her, and how she had given birth in a miraculous way.

Refrain: Praise to You, Lord, at whose coming
sinners turned from their wickedness
and entered into the protection
of the Garden of Eden, which is the holy Church.

1. At the birth of the Son, light shone out
   and darkness fled from the world;
   the universe lit up in praise
   of the Father's Radiance who had illuminated it.

2. He shone forth from the Virgin's womb
   and shadows vanished as He appeared:
   darkness and error were suffocated thereby,
   while earth's extremities were illumined in praise.

3. Among the Peoples* a great commotion arose
   for light had shone out in the dark.
   Nations leapt up in joyous praise
   of Him whose birth had given them light.

4. As His light flashed forth over the East
   Persia was illumined by the star
   which came down bearing her an invitation
   to come to the Epiphany that gladdens all.

5. The luminary speeded on its way to shine out
   amongst those in dark, summoning
   the Peoples to come and take pleasure
   in the great Light who had come down to earth.

ܩܘܡܼܚܡܶܐ ܕܥܲܠ ܥܲܢܝܼܕܹܐ ܡܗܲܝܡܢܹܐ

ܠܚܘܼܫܵܐ ܗ݇ܘܸܚܝܵܐ ܟܲܪ ܚܲܙܸܐ ܘܲܚܫܲܠܵܠܲܗܲܪ
ܗܹܐ ܣܲܗܿܕܵܐ ܗܿܘ ܟܵܘܟ݂ܵܘܲܐ݇
ܘܟܸܠܹܗ ܦܲܐܬܹܠܵܐܘܸܗ ܕܓܲܢܼܵܐ ܚܲܕ݇ܬ݁ܵܐ
ܘܲܐܸܫܠܼܡ ܟܲܪܠܵܐ ܦܿܪܼܫܵܠܲܬ܀

1. ܠܡܸܟܩܵܪܲܗ ܘܲܚܕܵܐ ܢܼܗܵܘܹܲܐ ܘܢܼܠܲܢ
ܩܲܚܘܪܸܗ ܫܸܥܬ݁ܵܐ ܗ݇ܝ ܚܸܠܟ݂ܐ܂
ܕܢܼܗܵܘܸ݁ܵܐ ܐܿܢܸܝܐܹܐ ܘܸܠܡܸܚܹܫܢܸܘܹܗ܄
ܚܙܼܪܚܼܸܗ ܘܸܐܬ݂ܵܐ ܕܗܼܵܲܘ ܐܸܬܸܼܘܲܘܲܚ܀

2. ܘܢܼܠܲܪ ܗܝ ܟ݂ܪܲܗܵܐ ܘܲܚܕܿܘܲܚܠܵܐ
ܘܩܼܗܘܪܲܗ ܢܲܓ݂ܠܵܐ ܟܼܪ ܐܿܠܲܡܢܼܪܲܪ܂
ܘܫܹܥܛܼܵܐ ܘܹܦܵܘܚܲܒܿ ܬܼܗ ܐܲܠܲܣܛܸܗ
ܩܲܕܼܘܲܘܲܗ ܗܹܩܘܩܵܐ ܘܸܢܚܹܚܫܸܗ܀

3. ܚܵܟ݂ܲܡܗܵܐ ܙܘܼܕ݂ܵܐ ܙܘܲܚܵܐ ܗܘܵܐ
ܘܲܚܫܸܥܼܘܲܘܕ݂ܵܐ ܢܼܗܵܘܹܲܐ ܘܢܼܠܸܪ܂
ܘܘܵܪܸܒ݂ ܐܵܢܩܿܡܠܵܐ ܘܸܢܥܹܟ݂ܒ݂ܒܲܝ
ܚܵܘܵܗ ܘܸܚܸܡܟ݂ܪܲܗ ܬܲܘܿܘܒܼ ܬ݁ܟܸܘܗ܀

4. ܐܿܪܼܟܼܐܝ ܢܼܗܵܘܵܘܹܗ ܟܸܠܐ ܚܲܪܼܫܵܐ
ܘܢܼܗܵܘܹܵܐ ܩܼܘܲܪܲܗ ܗ݇ܝ ܟ݂ܵܘܲܚܠܵܐ܂
ܘܢܸܫܸܚ ܩܲܚܲܙ݂ܗ ܐܘܸ ܐܲܚܚܸܗ
ܘܐܼܐܠܼܠܲܐ ܚܲܪܼܫܵܐ ܟܲܘܼܪܼܹܣ ܚܿܒ݂ܠܐ܀

5. ܘܿܩ݇ܠܝ ܢܼܩܲܡܿܪܼܐ ܩܿܐܐܼܐܠܵܐ ܘܢܼܠܲܢ
ܟ݂ܸܡ ܫܸܡܩܘܬܼܵܐ ܩܸܡܸܪܵܐ ܚܲܘܹܗܚ܂
ܘܢܸܐܠܲܐܘ݁ ܟ݂ܸܡܩܼܡܵܐ ܘܢܼܲܚܼܚܚܸܡܫܼܲܘܼ܂
ܚܼܢܼܗܵܘܸܘܵܘܐ ܙܘܼܟ݂ܐ ܘܲܐܼܘܿܒܼܟ݂ܐ ܢܸܫܸܚ܀

6. A single messenger, the star, came down Matt 2:2
   to announce and proclaim the glad tidings
   to the people of Persia, bidding them prepare,
   for the King whom they should worship had now
       shone forth.

7. Glorious Assyria*, once it was aware,
   summoned the Magi, instructing them:
   Take offerings and go to honour
   the great King who has shone forth in Judah.

8. The chiefs of Persia, in great delight,
   carried offerings from their country
   to bring to the Virgin's Son
   Gold, Myrrh and Frankincense. Matt 2:11

9. They entered to find Him a young baby
   living in a poor woman's house.
   They knelt down in joyful adoration Matt 2:11
   as they offered Him their treasures.

10. MARY: To what purpose are these?, Mary said,
    Why, and for what reason
    are you come from your own country
    with your treasures for this baby?

11. MAGI: Your son is a King, the Magi replied.
    He wears the crown and is Lord of all;
    his rule extends over the world
    and all are subject to his realm.

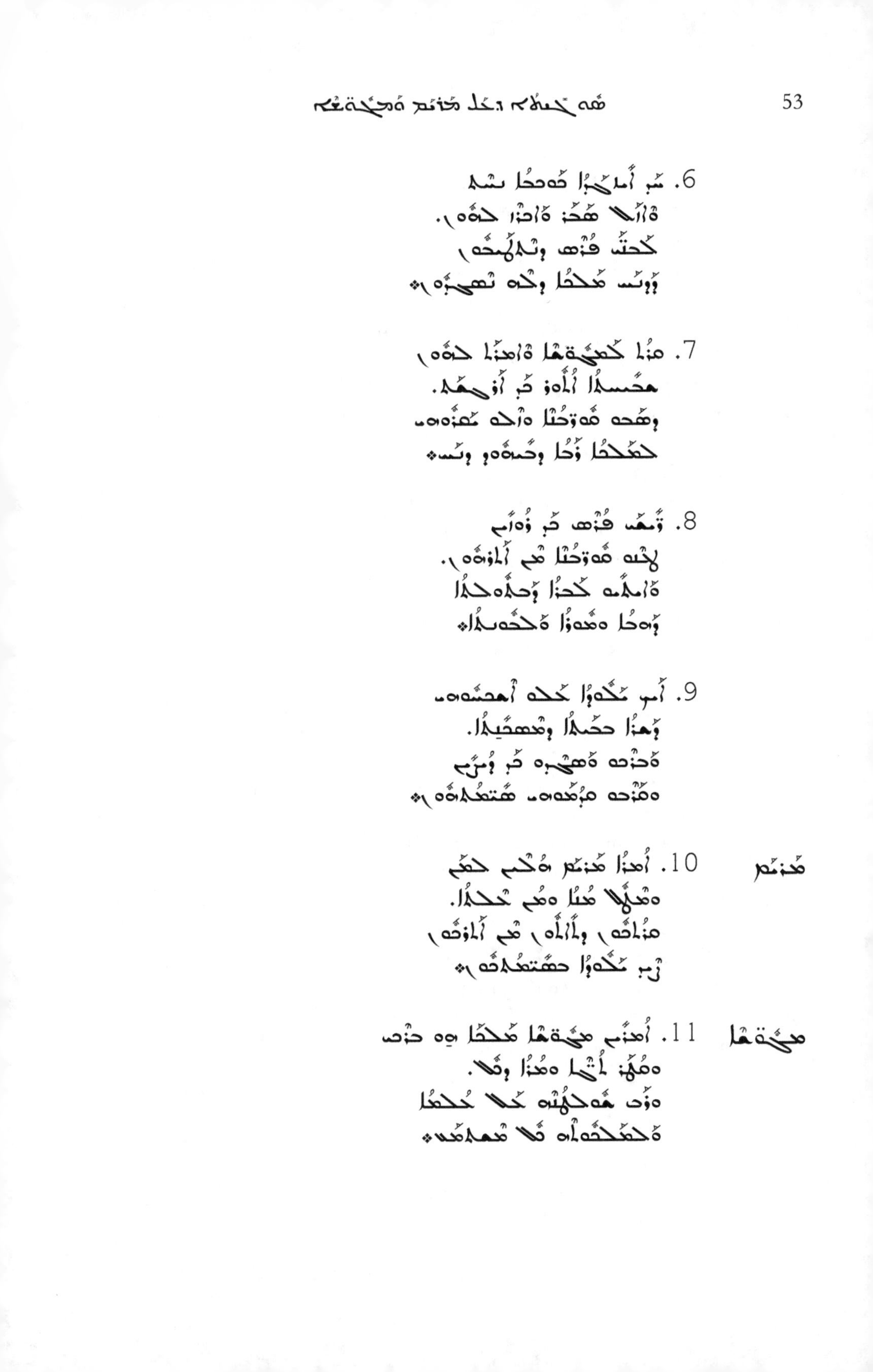

12. MARY: When has it ever happened
    that a poor girl should have given birth to a king?
    I am destitute and needy,
    how can a king appear from me?

13. MAGI: With you alone has this happened,
    for in you a great King shall appear.
    Through him your poverty shall make good,
    for crowns, O Mary, shall be subject to your son.

14. MARY: I have no royal treasure house,
    I have not ever met with wealth.
    The house is poor and the dwelling bare;
    don't proclaim to me that my son is a king.

15. MAGI: Your son is the great treasure house
    containing wealth sufficient to make all rich.
    Other kings' treasure stores will be reduced to poverty,
    but his will never run out or need to be rationed.

16. MARY: Maybe it is another king that you are talking about,
    born somewhere else: go and find out,
    for this is but the child of a poor girl
    who is unfitted to look on a king.

17. MAGI: How could we ever lose our way
    once the light was shining brightly?
    It was not darkness that bade us leave,
    but we have travelled in the light, and your son is the King.

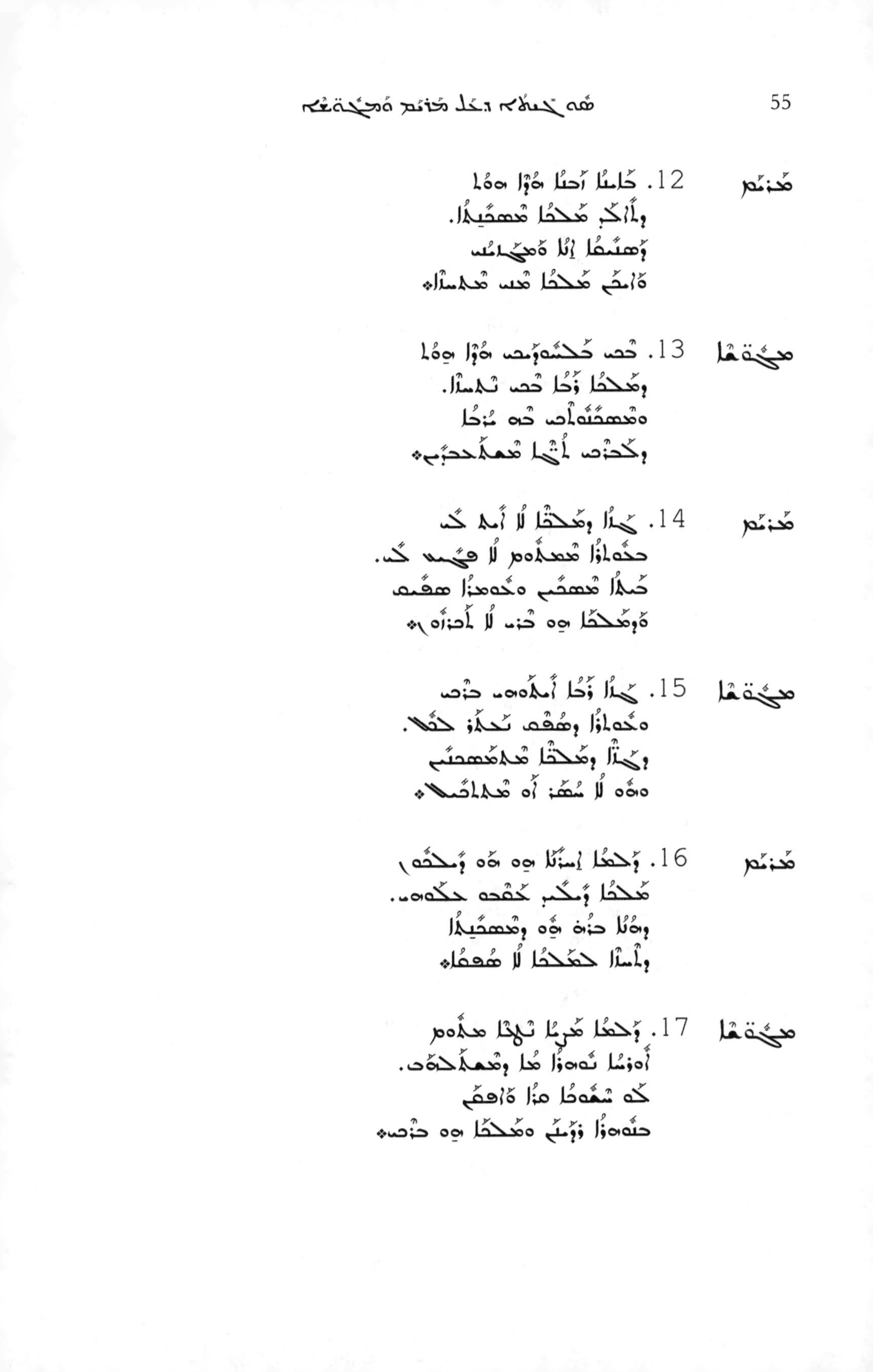

18. MARY: You can see the baby lying quiet
    and his mother's house, destitute and bare:
    there is nothing regal here,
    how can a king be seen here?

19. MAGI: Yes, we can see the child lying there
    quiet in gentle humility, as you say,
    but we can see too that he illumines the stars
    on high so that they announce him.

20. MARY: You should enquire of different people
    to find out who is the king, and then pay him homage.
    Maybe the path's direction has changed,
    and the king is some other child who has been born.

21. MAGI: My girl, you should accept this,
    for we have learnt that your son is the King.
    He directed us on a smooth path
    by means of a bright star, one that is not transient.

22. MARY: The child is small; he has
    no royal crown or throne.
    What is it that you have seen, that you offer
    your treasures as though to a king?

23. MAGI: He is small because he so willed it:
    the child is gentle and of low estate—until he is revealed:
    then will come the time when every crown
    shall be bowed down in worship of him.   Cp. Phil 2:10

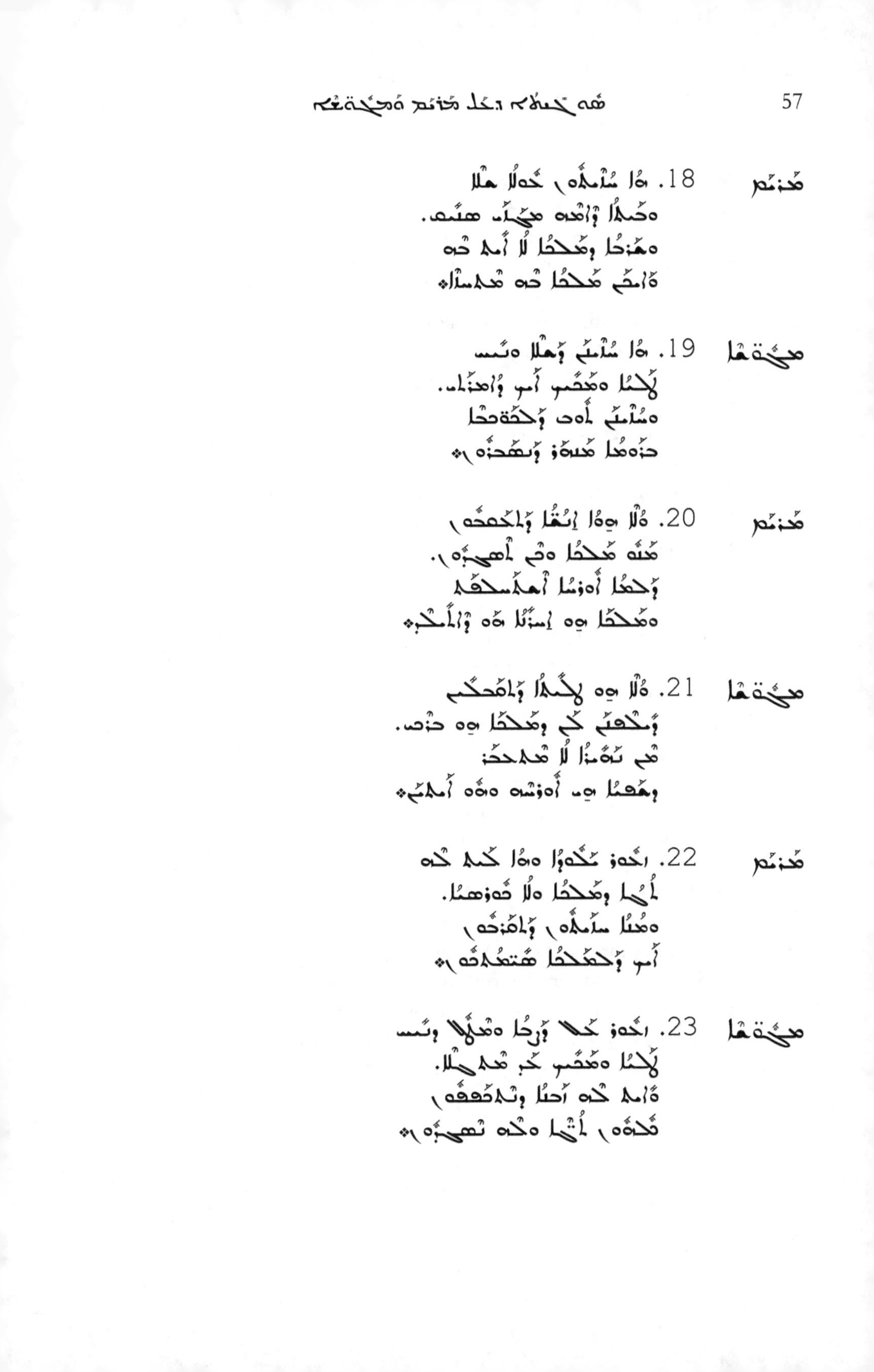

24. MARY: My son has no armies
or serried legions at his beck;   cp. Matt 26:53
he is content with his mother's poverty.
Why should he be proclaimed king by you?

25. MAGI: Your son's armies are aloft,
riding on high, all aflame,
and ever since one from them came and summoned
   us
our whole region has been astir.

26. MARY: The child is but a baby; how is it possible
he should be king over all the world?
How can a mere toddler
govern mighty men and renowned?

27. MAGI: Your child is old, young girl,
the Ancient of days*, prior to all others   Dan 7:13
Adam is younger by far than he,
and by him all creation is governed.

28. MARY: It would be best if you would explain
and throw light on all this affair.
Who has revealed to you this secret concerning my
   son,
that he is king in your country?

29. MAGI: It would be best if you would just accept it,
for if it had not been the truth that brought us,
we would never have come laden all the way here
from the ends of the earth for the sake of your son.

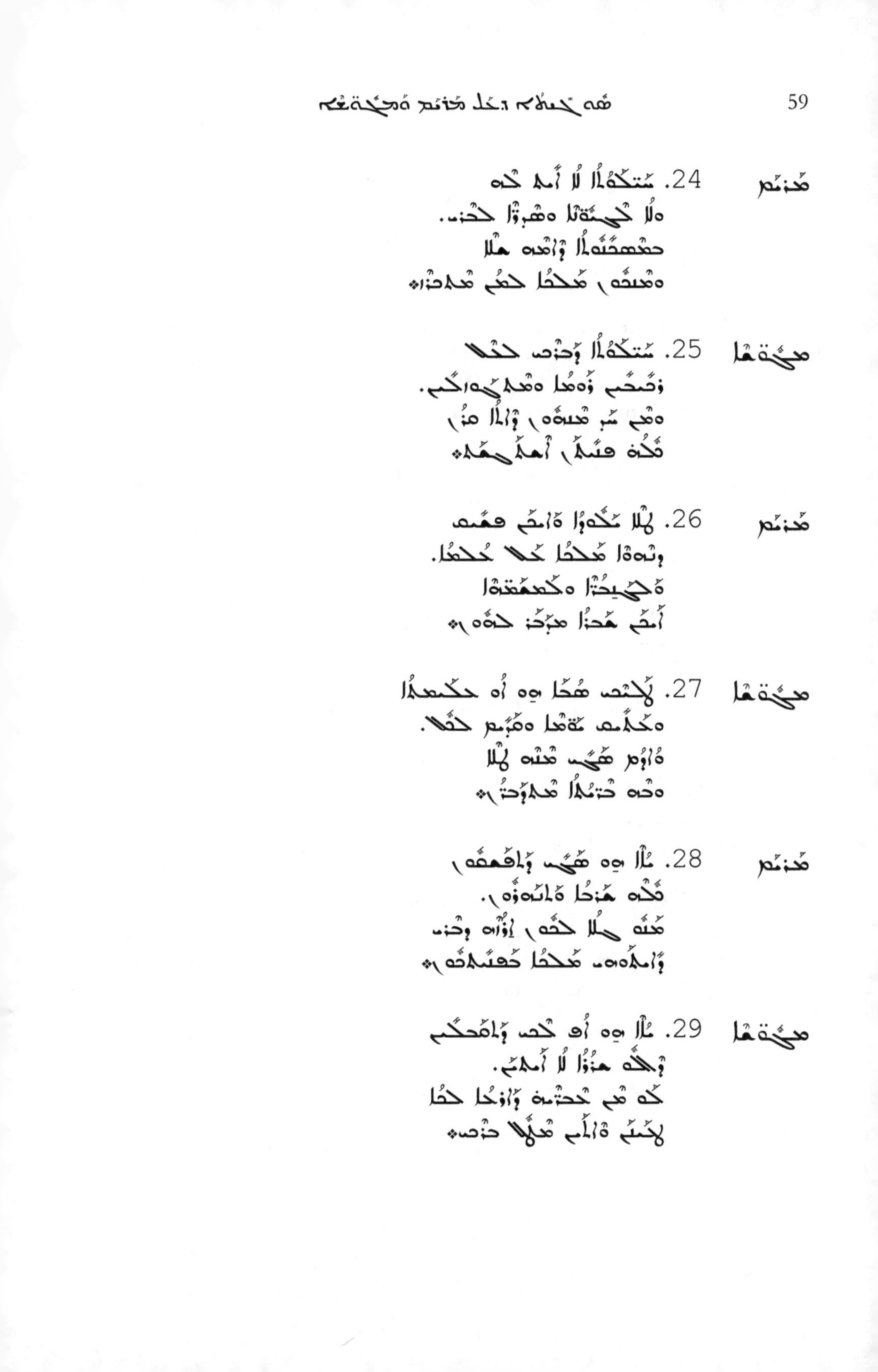

30. MARY: This whole secret, and what happened to you
    there in your country,
    please disclose it to me, like good friends:
    who summoned you to come to me here?

31. MAGI: A great star appeared to us,   Matt 2:2
    more glorious by far than the rest.
    Our land was enflamed with its light
    as it proclaimed that the King had shone forth.

32. MARY: I would not like you to tell all this
    in our country lest the local kings
    get to hear of it and become incensed
    with the child, out of envy.

33. MAGI: Do not be disturbed, young girl,
    your son will topple all crowns
    and place them beneath his feet.
    They cannot harm him, even if they get envious.

34. MARY: It is because of Herod that I am perturbed,   cp. Matt 2:3
    lest that mad dog upset me
    by unsheathing his sword
    and cutting off this sweet cluster* before it is ripe.   Isa 65:8

35. MAGI: Of Herod there is no need for you to fear;
    his throne lies in your child's hands:
    once it slips, his crown will totter and fall;
    he will be destroyed, and that is the end of the wretch!

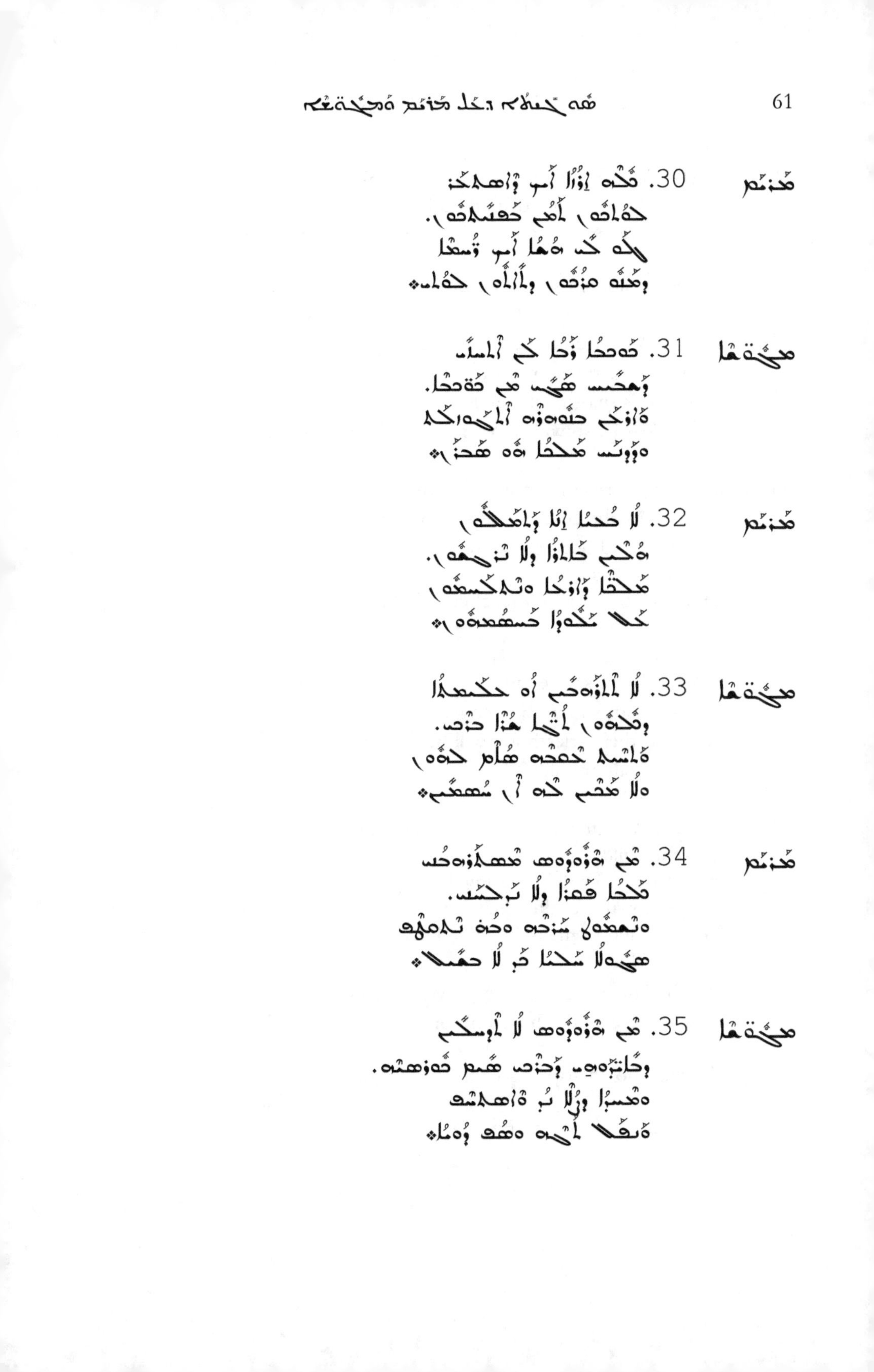

36. MARY: Jerusalem will be a torrent of blood   cp. Matt 2:16
    as lovely children are disfigured by him;
    if the city gets to know of it, people will make a dash for him.
    Let our talk be in secret: do not cause a disturbance.

37. MAGI: All torrents and awesome gorges
    will be pacified by your son.
    Jerusalem's sword will be blunted,
    and, unless he so wills it, your son will not be killed.

38. MARY: Jerusalem's scribes and priests
    are well instructed in matters of blood:
    if they should become aware, they will stir up murderous feuds
    directed at me and the child. O Magi, please keep quiet.

39. MAGI: These scribes and priests have no power
    to harm your son in their envy:
    by him is their priesthood will be dissolved,
    their festivals annulled.

40. MARY: A watcher revealed to me when I conceived the child
    that 'Your son will be a King   Luke 1:32–33
    whose crown is exalted, never to be removed'.
    He intimated to me just as you have said.

41. MAGI: That watcher, then, of whom you speak
    must be the one who summoned us, looking like a star.
    He was shown to us, so that we might announce to you
    that your son is greatly more glorious than the stars.

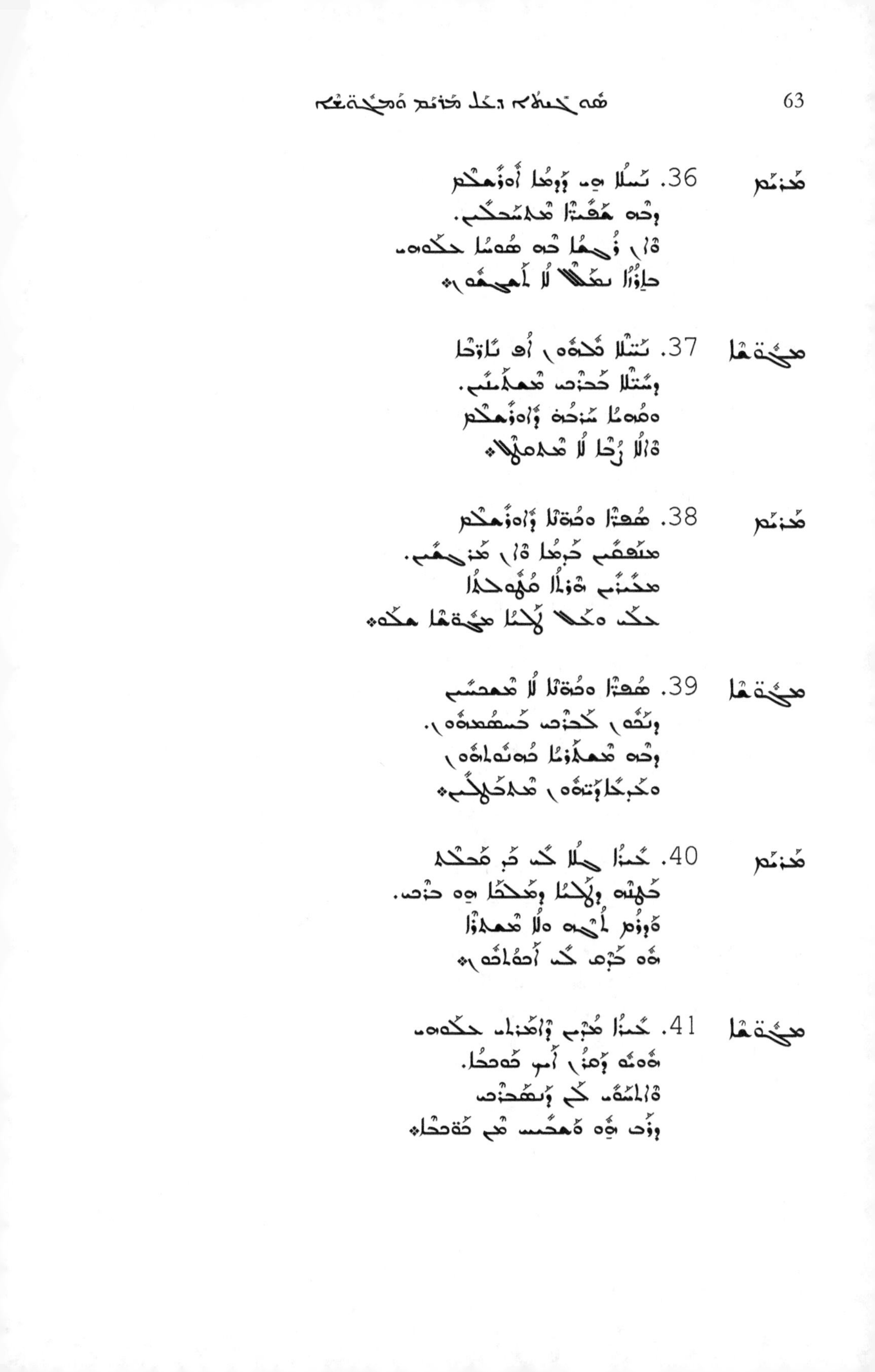

42. MARY: That angel who appeared to me
 explained to me, when he announced it,
 that his kingdom would have no end,   Luke 1:33
 but I kept it a secret, so that it might not be revealed.

43. MAGI: That star, too, explained to us
 how your son would wear the crown.
 Its appearance was different,
 for it was an angel, though it never told us so.

44. MARY: When the watcher announced this to me
 he called him his Lord, even though he had not yet been conceived;   Luke 1:28
 he proclaimed him to me as the Son of the Most High,   Luke 1:32
 but where his Father is, I have no idea.

45. MAGI: The star too proclaimed to us
 that he who is born is the Lord of the heights:
 your son rules over the luminaries
 and without his orders they do not shine.

46. MARY: I will reveal before you a further secret
 so that you may be reassured:
 I gave birth to my son in virgin wise.
 Since he is God's Son, go and proclaim him as such.   Luke 1:35

47. MAGI: That star has already taught us
 that he is God's Son and is Lord.
 Your son is above all things,
 for your child is exalted above all worlds.

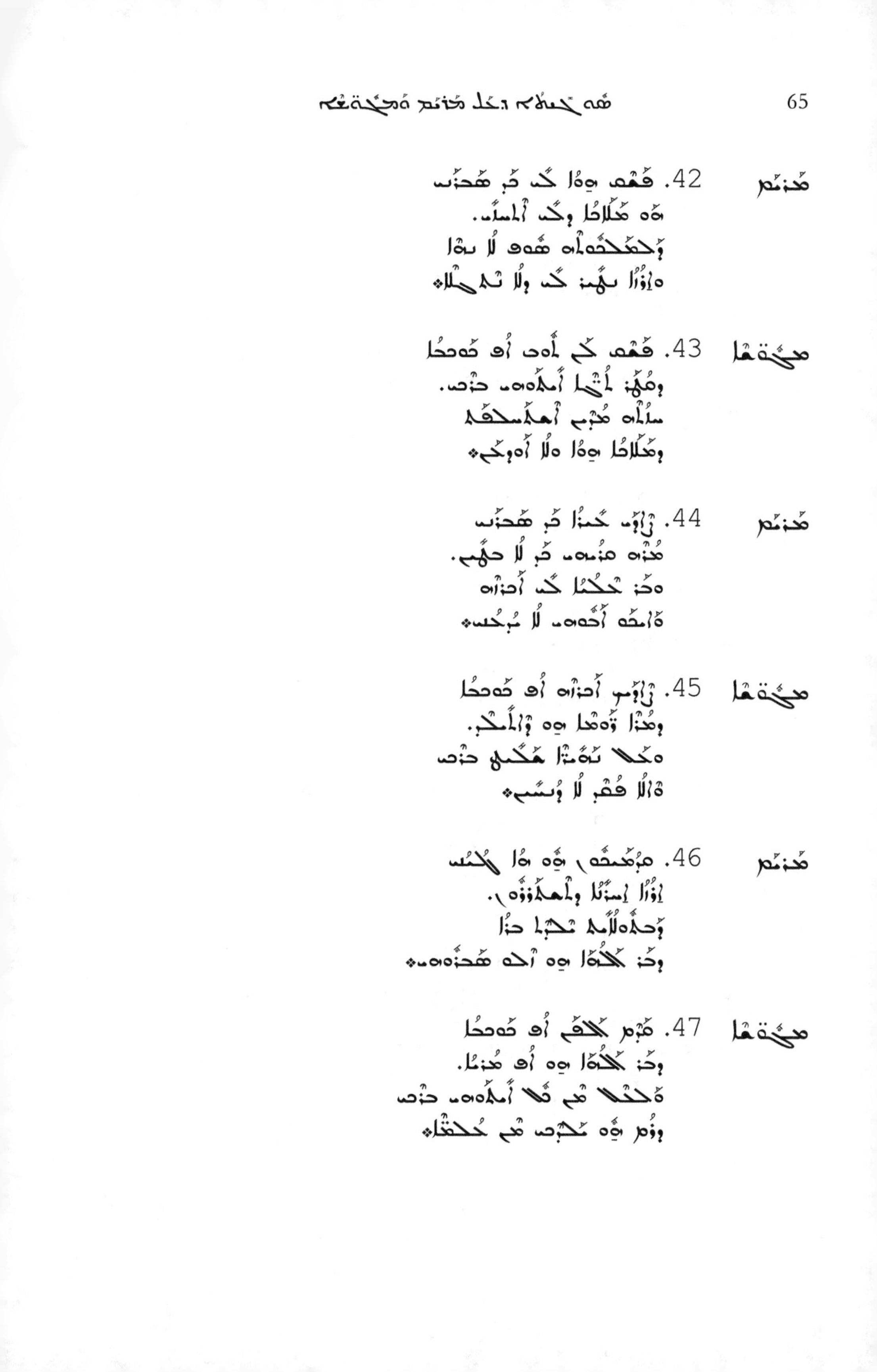

48. MARY: The heights and depths testify concerning him,
    along with all watchers and stars,
    that he is Son of God and Lord.
    Convey the news of him to your country.

49. MAGI: The heavenly height, by means of one star,
    put Persia into commotion, and she has believed
    that your son is the great King
    to whom all nations are subject.

50. MARY: Convey back peace to your lands;
    may prosperity abound in your realm.
    O apostles of truth, may you be believed
    in every place through which you travel.

51. MAGI: The peace of your son shall convey us
    safe back to our country, just as we came.
    When his rule takes hold of the world,
    may he visit our land and sanctify it!

52. MARY: May Persia rejoice at the tidings you bring;
    may Assyria exult at your arrival.
    Once the Kingdom of my son has shone out,
    may he place his standard in your land!

53. Let the Church exult and sing
    praise at the birth of the Most High,
    for both heights and depths stand illumined at His Epiphany.
    Blessed is He at whose birth all receive joy!

	48.
	49.
	50.
	51.
	52.
	53.

IV–V. MARY AND THE GARDENER

The risen Christ and Mary (John 20):
two anonymous dialogue poems.

Both these dialogues take as their starting point the resurrection narrative in John 20:15–16, where Mary encounters the risen Christ whom, however, she takes to be the gardener. In St John's Gospel the Mary in question is identified as Mary Magdalene (John 20:18), but a widespread early Syriac tradition identified the Mary of this episode as Mary the mother of Jesus. This is the case in both these poems, as can be seen from the words '*my* Son' in the second stanza of IV, and from the final stanza of V, 'Blessed is the Son of the Living one ... who showed to *His mother* that He is the Shepherd'. In V, Mary's repeated reference to her 'beloved' will carry deliberate resonances of the Song of Songs.

IV. Mary and the Gardener (East Syriac poem)

1. On Sunday, in the morning early   John 20:1
   along came Mary to the tomb.

2. MARY: Who will show me, she was saying,
   my Son* and my Lord for whom I am seeking?

3. As the Gardener did our Lord appear
   to her, answering and speaking to her thus:

4. GARDENER: Disclose to me, o lady, what it is
   that you are seeking today in this garden.   John 20:15

5. MARY: O Gardener, please do not refuse me,
   do not drive me from your garden.

6. It is a single fruit that is mine;
   apart from it there is nothing else that I seek.

7. GARDENER: At this season you should realize
   that no fruits are to be found in any garden;

8. so how is it that you are telling me
   that you are looking for fruit today?

9. MARY: You should know, O Gardener,
   that the fruit for which I am searching

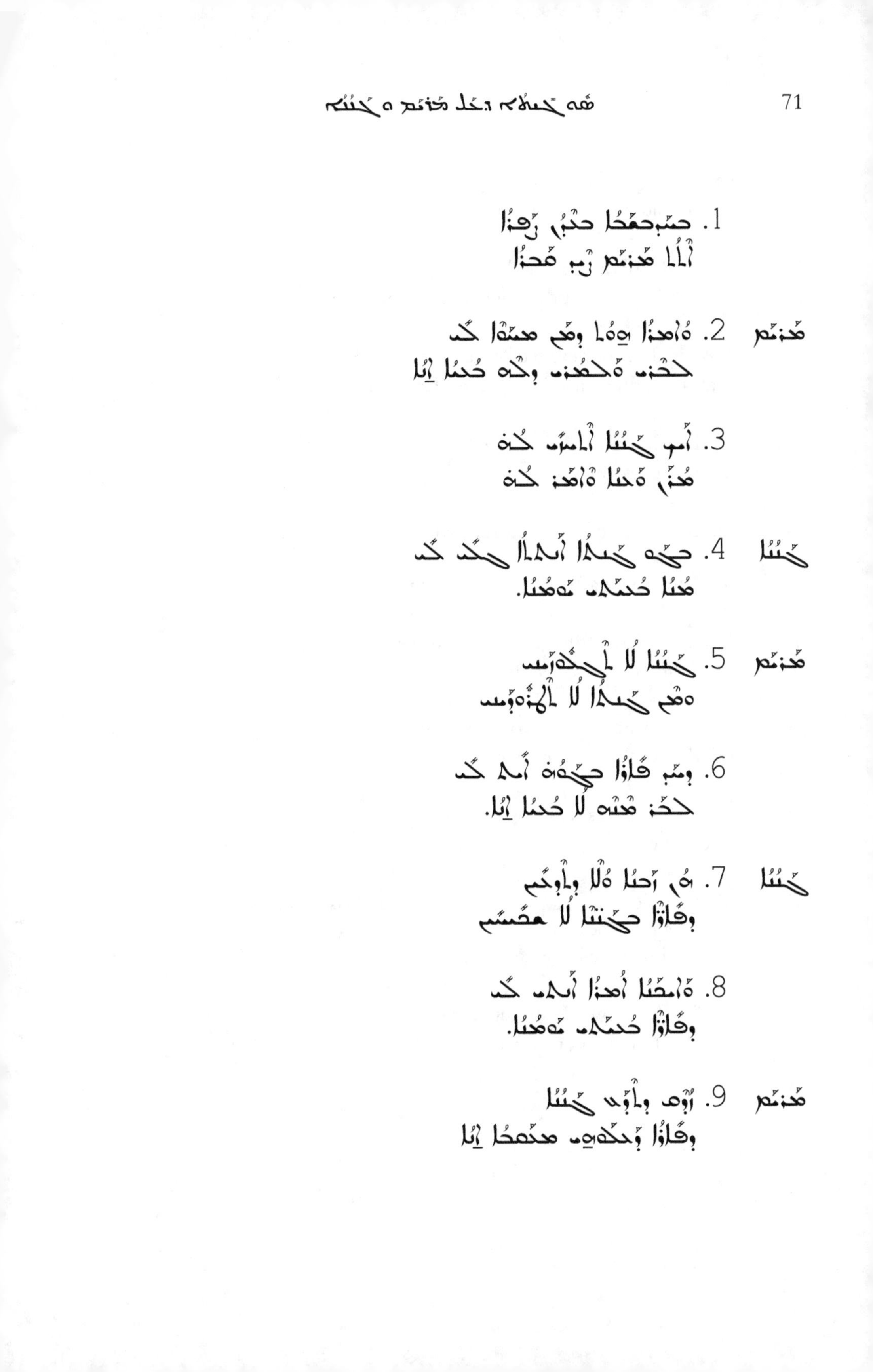

10. will give me life—such is my hope—
    if I should but happen to see it.

11. GARDENER: What is this fruit, young lady,
    about which you speak such amazing words?

12. MARY: I know very well and am quite certain
    that the sight of it is too exalted for the eye.

13. GARDENER: How you weary me with your talk,
    how you vex me with what you say.

14. MARY: Where have you removed him? Disclose this to me,
    for I am going after him, seeking him.

15. GARDENER: Why, lady, do you seek
    the living in Sheol, the devourer*?   Luke 24:5

16. He concerning whom you are asking
    left the tomb this very night

17. while the guards were wielding swords,
    resembling raving dogs.

18. MARY: Concerning his resurrection disclose and explain to me
    so that I may be believing in him.

19. For he flew down from highest heaven
    and dwelt in a virgin womb.

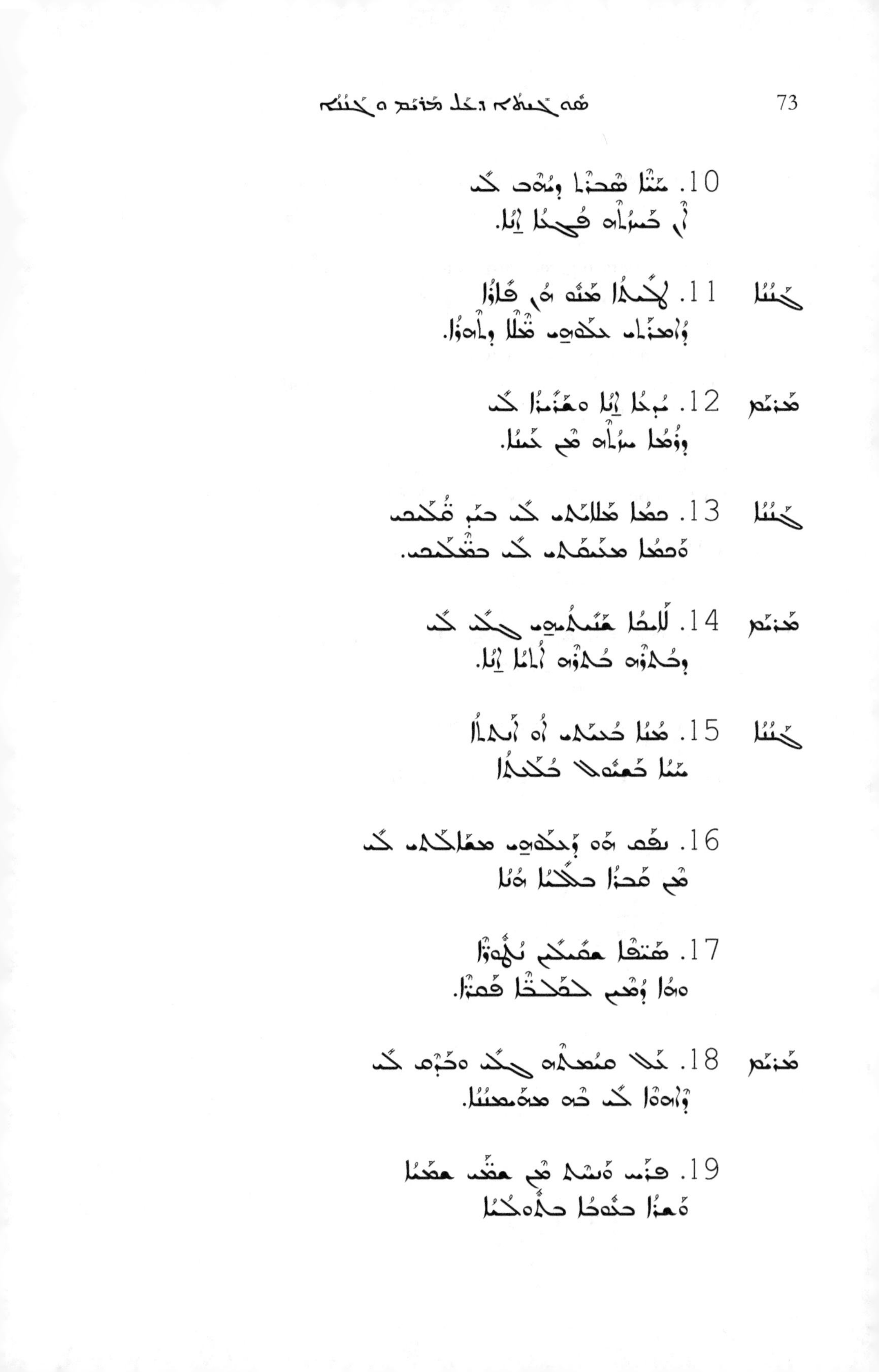

20. GARDENER: Incline your ear, O woman, and listen,
    so that I may be the one to show you concerning him.

21. His resurrection gives witness to her who bore him,
    his mother gives witness to his resurrection*;

22. Height and depth are my witnesses
    that, transcending nature, he was both born and now
         has risen.

23. —She heard his voice and recognized him,
    for he repeated the words 'Mary, Mary'*.   John 20:16

24. MARY: Come to me, my Lord and my Master*,
    for now I forget my anguish.

25. —Come in your compassion, O Son of Mary,
    just as you came to Mary,

26. and with you, at your resurrection, let your light shine
         forth
    on me and on him who composed this*.

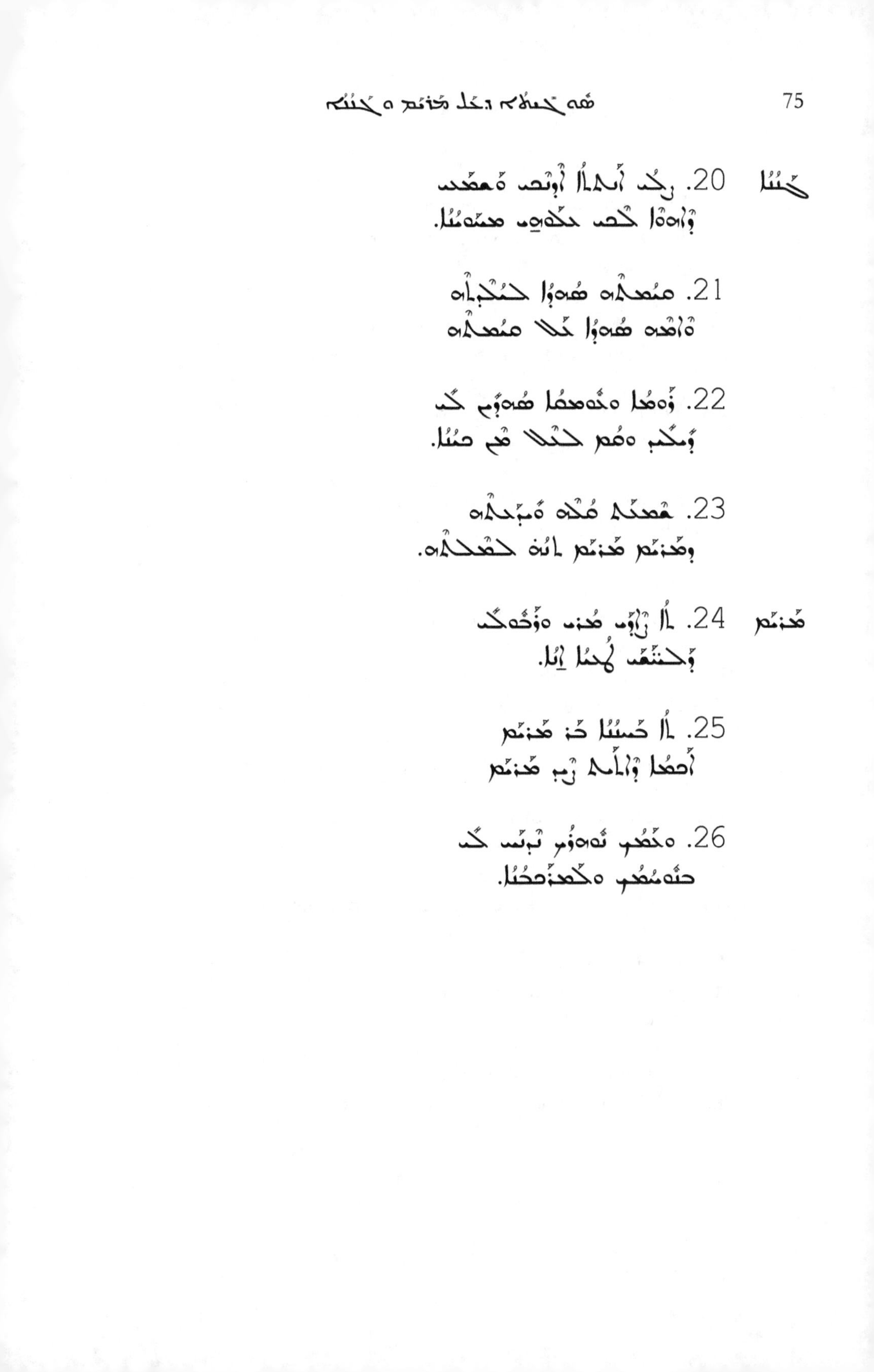

V. Mary and the Gardener (West Syriac poem)

1. MARY: O Guardian who guards the garden,
   show me the way by which my beloved went.

2. JESUS: O young woman, do not seek here
   for your master, for he went off hence in the night.

3. MARY: I beg you, O Guardian of the garden,
   show me the way my beloved went.

4. JESUS: This night he took his rest with me,
   but he has set off from here; why do you stand thus?

5. MARY: O Gardener, take a reward for your words,
   just show me where are his tracks.

6. JESUS: He has left the garden and gone off outside;
   why are you asking after his tracks here?

7. MARY: Show me his footprint, so that I can go after him;
   come, show me, and then stay in your garden.

8. JESUS: His footprint is here, why do you ask?
   The person you are seeking has left and gone outside.

9. He was lying here in this garden
   all of yesterday, the one whom you are seeking, young woman.

10. He was lying here in this garden,
    but he has gone off hence, so why do you stand thus?

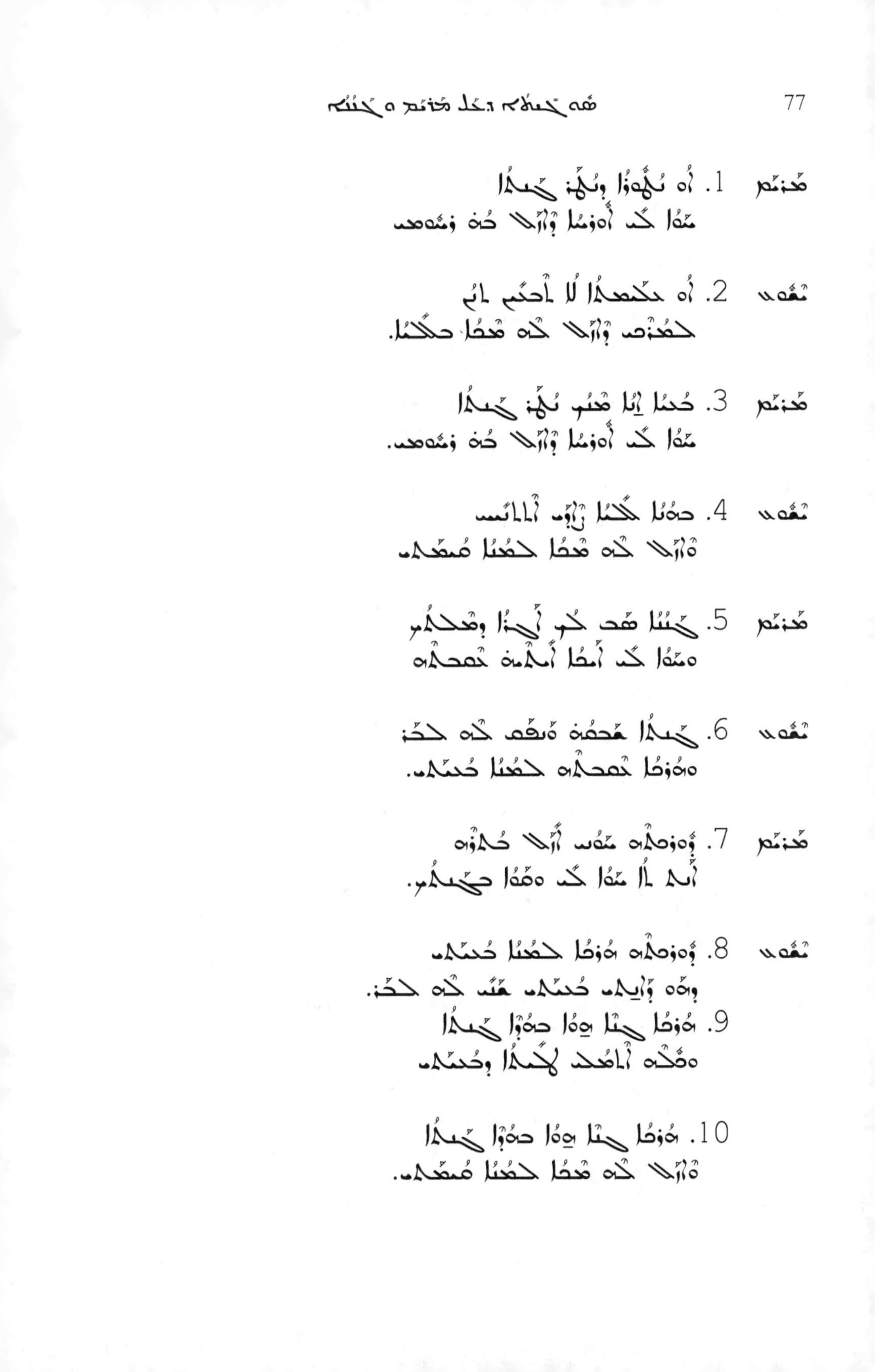

11. MARY: Then what should I do, for I have lost my beloved?
    Where has he gone, so that I may seek him, in case he may be found?

12. What did he say to you when he left,
    O Gardener, owner of the garden?

13. The time is short for me to look for my lord,
    seeing that my sight has been deprived of his beauty.

14. JESUS: Go off, woman; don't stand here with me,
    for I am just the keeper in this garden.

15. MARY: Show the way that I may go after him;
    come, show me, and then stay in your garden.

16. JESUS: I have shown you the way, and the gate to the garden;
    come, woman, leave and search for your beloved.

17. MARY: I am greatly distressed if you do not tell
    where I should go to look for my beloved whom I have lost.

18. JESUS: Young woman, be persuaded and accept what I have said:
    the person you are looking for has gone off outside.

19. MARY: I know, sir, that he has gone off outside,
    and that he is not where he was lying in the evening.

20. JESUS: A whole day he rested beside me,
    but he has gone off from here, so why do you stand thus?

ܗܘ ܟܝܢܐ ܕܒܪ ܐܢܫܐ ܘ ܟܢܝܗ

مُحَنَّمَ 11. ومُحَد أَحْدٍ إِنَّا وَكَنَبْعَدِي أَوجَدًا
ةَانَعًا أَرَّلَا أَحَنَدوي وَلَحْعًا هَعْدَكَبَ.

12. ومُحَد أَهُدَٰ كَمِ مَ أَرَّلَا كَه
أَه كَحِنَا وَهُدَرَه وَكَىٰدًا.

13. ذِكْدَو هَو كَه ذَحُنَا وَأَحْنَدوي حُدُرَى
كَحَا هُم وَٱاكَحُدًا سَامَ هَمِ هُوهِرَه.

ىَقُومـ 14. ذِك كَحَ أَيَحَاْا لَا اَقُوهَي حَكَه
وَنَهُورًا أَحَكَ دَهُوْا كَحَدًا.

مُحَنَّمَ 15. مَنَّمَ أَوزَنَا أَرَّلَا كَمَرَه
أَي لَا مَنَا كَه وَهَنَا حَكَحَيَ.

ىَقُومـ 16. مَنَّمَكَحَ أَوزَنَا وَأَوحَا وَكَحَدًا
أَه أَيَحَاْا لَمِ قُومَ ةَحَد وَسَقَحَ.

مُحَنَّمَ 17. لَحِ مَنَّمَ كَه ٱلَا أَهَدَنَا كَه
أَنَعًا أَرَّلَا أَحَنَدوي كَنَبْعَدِي وَأَوجَدًا.

ىَقُومـ 18. لَحَكَا ٱلَاقَمَى وَهَحَد هَحَكَا
وَهَ وَكَه حُنَكَ هَنَ كَه حَحَر.

مُحَنَّمَ 19. مَرِكَا إِنَا هُدَى وَنَقَمَ كَه حَحَر
وَلَا أَحَوى أَنَعًا وَحَرَهَعَا حِنَا.

ىَقُومـ 20. مَوحَا هُكَه رَبَى ٱلَاىَى
ةَأَرَّلَا كَه هَحَا حَحُنَا مَحَكَى.

21. MARY: For the whole day I have gone out after him
    and news reached me that he had entered and was staying here.

22. JESUS: The whole night he was resting beside me,
    but he got up early and set off before the night was out.

23. MARY: No, by your life, O Guardian of the garden,
    I am not going to leave you without seeing my lord.

24. JESUS: Why are you going to court with me, woman,
    I am just a passer by in this garden.

25. MARY: I heard from you, and you yourself told me,
    that the garden is yours, so don't you know my lord?

26. JESUS: Because you saw me in this garden
    you imagined that the garden was mine.

27. MARY: You hold sway* over this garden,
    and for that reason you know what has happened.

28. JESUS: What sway in this garden should a passer by have
    who just came and spent the night?

29. MARY: I do obeisance, sir, have pity on me;
    take a reward and show me my lord.

30. JESUS: Your looks are very forward, woman,
    you seem to me to love that young man.

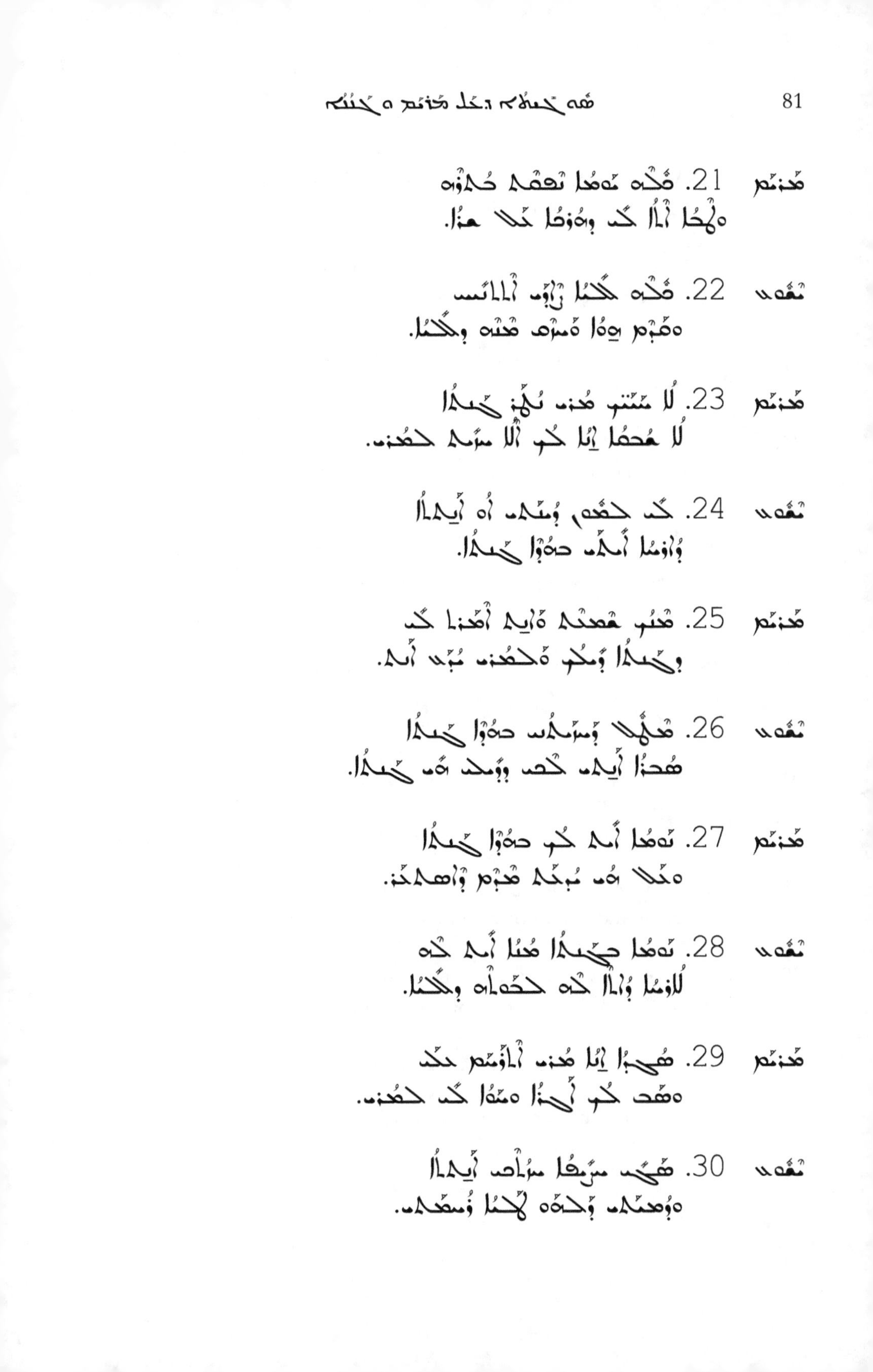

31. MARY: I am in grief over my lord whom I have lost;
    love for him is a burning fire.

32. JESUS: Because you have seen me here in the garden
    you imagine that the garden is mine.

33. MARY: Your very mouth, sir, testifies against you,
    that the garden is yours and that you know my lord.

34. JESUS: You show great boldness of speech
    because I have been speaking with you, woman.

35. MARY: Consent, sir, and be persuaded, accept my words,
    for my heart is burning, and that is why I have spoken.

36. JESUS: I have shown you my will, I have been patient with you
    and have spoken with you, woman.

37. MARY: I have called you by your name, why are you running away?
    I am not leaving you unless I have seen my lord.

38. Let your voice thunder out the truth in my ears
    concerning the one who came to you in the night.

39. Desire for my beloved is burning my heart
    and you, O Gardener, are adding to the fire.

40. JESUS: Give rest to your desire and remove your grief,
    for the one whom you are seeking is the person whom you see.

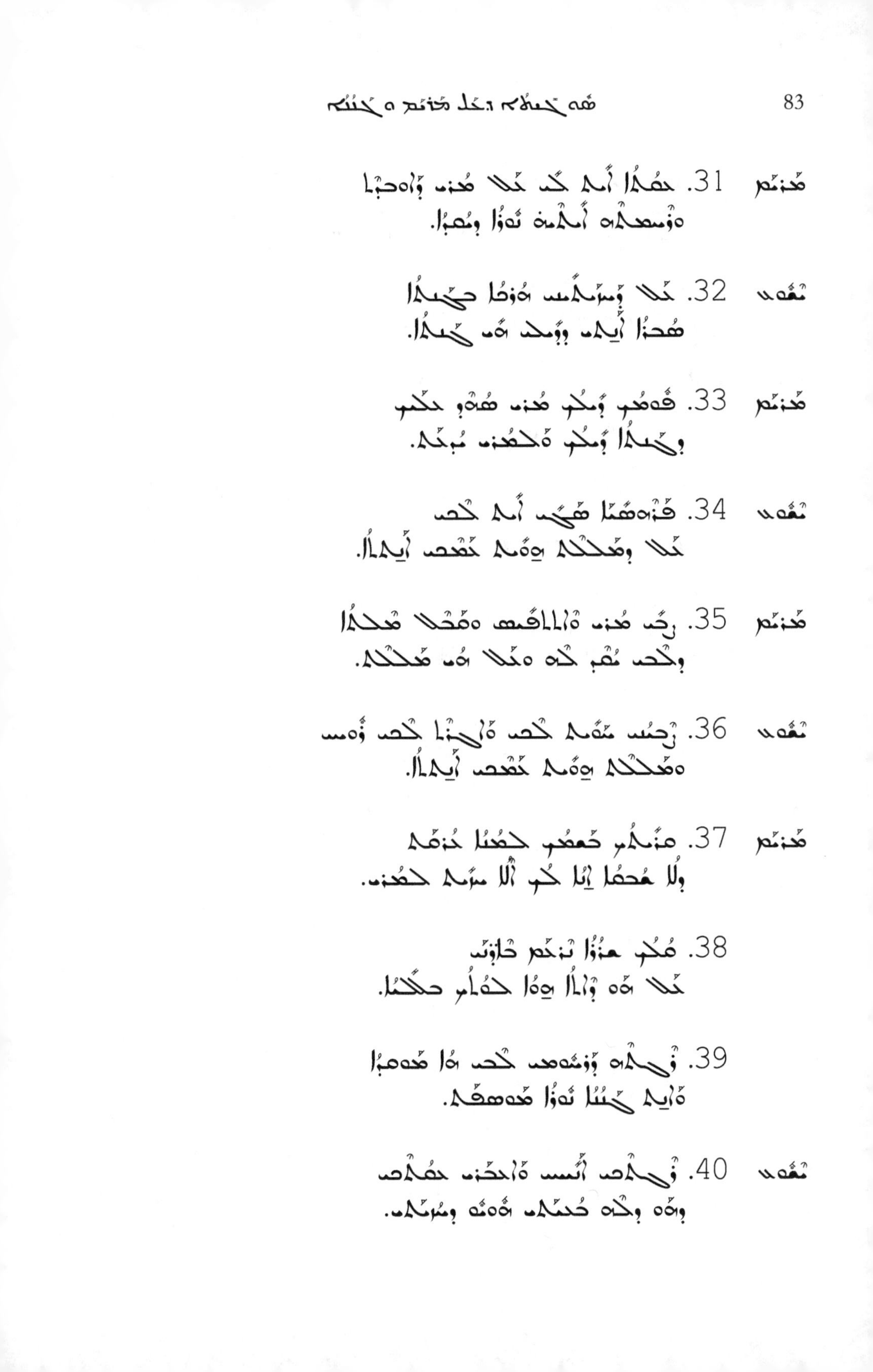

41. MARY: Peace to that mouth of yours, o Lord of his handmaid,
    which has revealed to me his self and had pity on me!

42. JESUS: Peace to you, Mary, remove your grief,
    and go in peace to look for my friends.

43. MARY: Come, Lord, and remove your friends' mourning,
    for they are all sitting in sorrow.

44. JESUS: I am going to the place where they are residing: Matt 28:10
    my brothers and friends will see me there.

45. —Blessed is the Son of the Living One who has arisen from the dead
    and shown to His mother that He is the Shepherd!

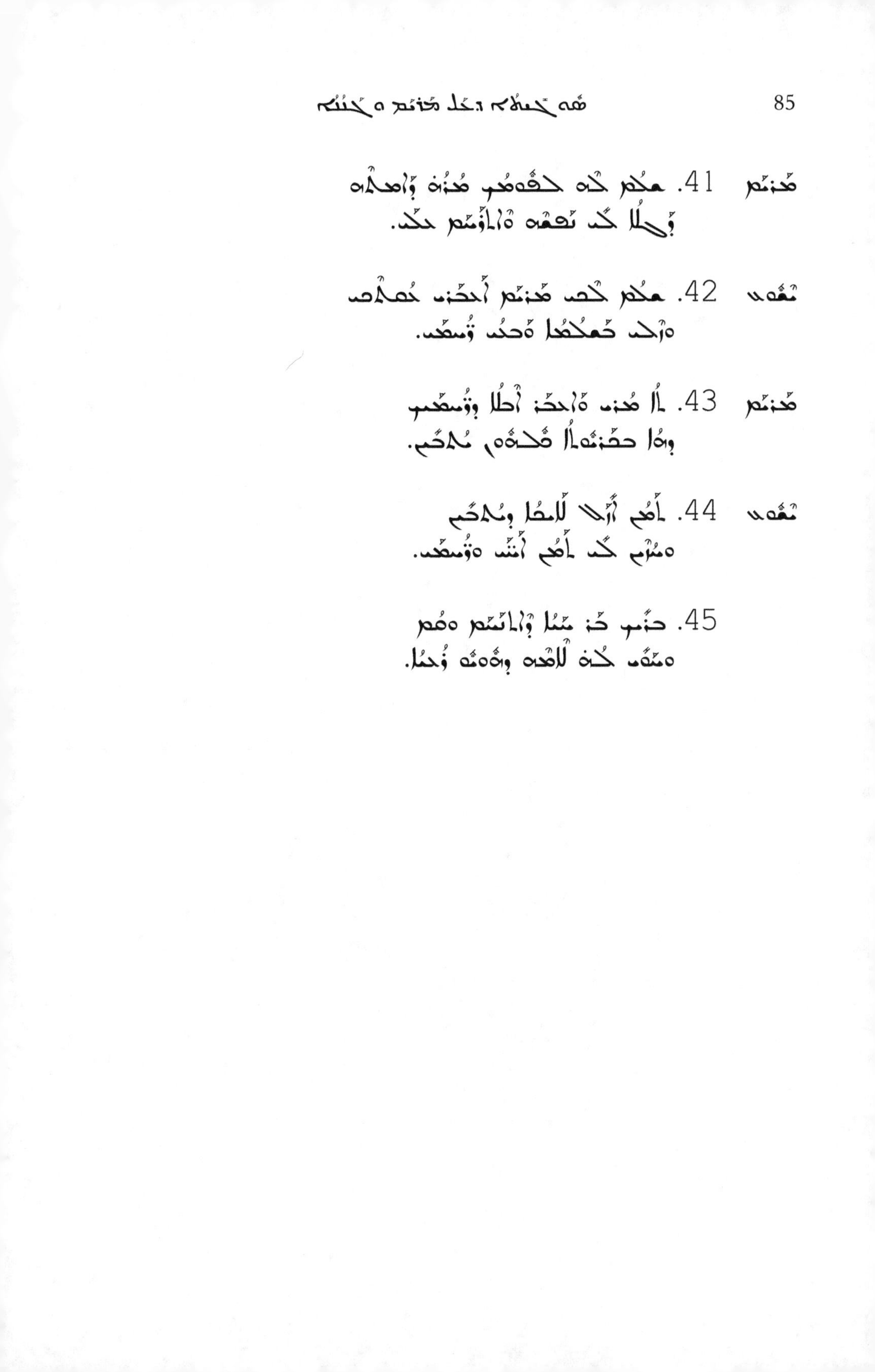

ANNOTATION

ABBREVIATIONS:

Bride of Light = Brock, S.P. *Bride of Light: Hymns on Mary from the Syriac Churches*. Piscataway, 2010.
Fire from Heaven = idem. *Fire from Heaven: Studies in Syriac Theology and Liturgy*. Variorum Reprints, 2006.
Holy Spirit = idem. *The Holy Spirit in the Syrian Baptismal Tradition*. Gorgias Liturgical Studies, 4. Piscataway NJ, ³2008.
Studies in Syriac Christianity = idem. *Studies in Syriac Christianity*. Variorum Reprints, 1992.

I. MARY AND THE ANGEL

I.1.1 <u>Power</u>: Syriac writers usually differentiate 'the Power of the Most High' in Luke 1:35 from 'the Holy Spirit' (who precedes it), and identify the Power instead as the divine Word.

<u>resided</u> (*shro*): in early Syriac writings this verb (often in combination with 'came down', as here) is regularly used in paraphrases of Luke 1:35, even though all the Syriac versions employ a different verb (*aggen*) there. It seems likely that *shra* represents the very earliest Syriac term used to denote the Incarnation (see *Fire from Heaven*, chap. X; and for *aggen* and its associations, chaps. XI–XIII).

I.1.2 <u>compelled by His love</u>: the phrase occurs in a number of other *sughyotho* (e.g. the Dialogue between the Sinful Woman and Satan, stanza 1).

I.2.1 <u>Son of the Bounteous One</u> (*bar 'atiro*): the title already features in Ephrem, *Madroshe* on the Nativity 15:3 and 19:2. The paradox of rich/poor is based on 2 Cor. 8:9.

I.2.2 <u>poor girl</u>: in Ephrem, *Madroshe* on the Nativity 19:13 Christ is called 'son of poor parents'.

I.4.1 <u>Lord of all</u> (*Moro d-kul*): the title already occurs in the Acts of Thomas (ed. Wright, pp. 177, 240) and Ephrem (*Madroshe* on Faith, 60:8). More common in Ephrem is the biblical *More kul* (Wisdom 6:7, 8:3 and Bar Sira 24:8), which is also attested in Palmyrene in an inscription dated AD 132 (Hillers, D.R., and E. Cussini, *Palestinian Aramaic Texts*. Baltimore/London, 1996, no. 0344 = CIS 3998).

I.4.3 <u>watchers</u> (*'ire*): this term for angels derives from Daniel 4:13; it is more frequent in early Syriac writers than its synonym *mal'ake*. See further Cramer, W. *Die Engelvorstellung bei Ephrem dem Syrer.* OCA 173; 1965.

I.5.3 <u>who bent down</u>: the verb is often used of the Incarnation in early writers (though it is absent from Aphrahat), e.g. Acts of Thomas (ed. Wright, p. 40), Ephrem, *Madroshe* against the Heresies 30:3.

I.7.1 <u>David's daughter</u>: thus already, Ephrem, *Madroshe* on the Nativity 2:13, 16.

I.8.1 <u>flew down</u> (*dol*): similarly in connection with the Incarnation in Ephrem, *Madroshe* on Faith 4:2.

I.9.1 <u>a letter</u>: Syriac poets make a great deal of use of letter imagery (e.g. *Bride of Light*, no. 25, which opens 'The Father wrote a letter and sent it at the hands of a watcher to Nazareth'). See further Brock, S.P. "Mary as a 'letter', and some other letter imagery in Syriac liturgical texts." *Vox Patrum* (Festschrift for M. Starowieyski) 26 (2006): 89–99.

I.9.4 <u>fair hope</u>: the words translate Greek *eudokia* in the Peshitta at Luke 2:14.

I.10.2 <u>destitute girl</u>: similarly in stanza 42, below; also Mary and Joseph, stanza 38, and Mary and the Magi, stanza 12.

I.11.4 <u>blessed the Fruit...</u>: the anonymous author inadvertently puts these words of Elizabeth (Luke 1:42) into Gabriel's mouth!

I.18.4 <u>her former glory</u>: according to Syriac tradition (inherited from Judaism), Adam and Eve were created clothed in a 'garment of glory'; this was lost at the Fall, but made available again to humanity by Christ: at baptism Christians put on this garment of glory (or, of light) in potential, but it only at the end of time does it become a reality, that is, for those who have preserved this garment (linked with the wedding garment of Matthew 22:11) in purity. For this theme, see further "Clothing metaphors as a means of theological expression in Syriac tradition," reprinted in *Studies in Syriac Christianity*, chap. XI, and "The Robe of Glory: a biblical image in the Syriac tradition." *The Way* 39 (1999): 247–59; *Holy Spirit*, 61–7.

I.20.4 <u>a divine being</u>: or 'goddess'. In his Commentary on Genesis (II.20) Ephrem states that, prompted by the Serpent, Eve (and Adam) had wanted to attain to divinity by eating of the forbidden fruit of the Tree of Knowledge: 'Because she had believed the Serpent, she ate first, imagining that she would come back clothed in divinity...'. In the Nisibene *Madroshe* (69:12) he writes, 'The Most High knew that Adam had wanted to become a god, so He sent His Son who put him on in order to grant him his desire' (Adam here represents humanity).

I.35.4: <u>over you the Holy Spirit will reside</u> (*shore*): at Luke 1:35 all the Syriac versions use a different verb (*naggen*); see the note to I.1.1.

I.37.3 <u>Second Heaven</u>: based on Isaiah 65:17, this became a frequent title for Mary in Patristic literature in every language.

I.48.1 <u>blessed is his name</u> (*brik shmeh*): it is interesting that this features as a divine title in several Palmyrene inscriptions (including the one cited at I.4.1).

II. Mary and Joseph

II.3.1 <u>child who fashions all</u>: *ṣo'ar kul*, 'Fashioner of all', is frequently found as a title of Christ in liturgical poetry.

II.3.2 <u>in her breasts was the milk</u>: the paradox of the Virgin who nevertheless provides milk is already found in Ephrem, *Madroshe* on the Nativity 11:4, 28:5.

II.14.4 <u>lamb from the branch</u>: the reference is to the ram caught in a branch, Genesis 22:13. In his Commentary on Genesis (section XX) Ephrem writes: 'That the ram had not been there (before) is testified by Isaac's question concerning the lamb; and that the tree had not been there is assured by the wood on Isaac's shoulders. The mountain burst forth with the tree, and the tree with the ram, so that, through the ram that was suspended on the tree and became the sacrifice instead of Abraham's son, that day of His (John 8:56) might be depicted, when He was suspended on the wood like the ram and tasted death on behalf of the whole world'. The miraculous 'birth' of the lamb subsequently came to be used as a typological parallel to Mary's virgin birthgiving.

II.16.2–3 <u>... issuing from Adam</u>: Eve's miraculous birth from Adam's rib was regularly taken as a typological parallel (in reverse, as it were) to Mary, the Second Eve, giving miraculous birth to Christ, the Second Adam.

II.22.3 <u>summon the local midwives</u>: this is based on traditions in the second-century Protogospel of James. Extensive use of this work will be found in the narrative poem on Joseph and Mary, translated in *Bride of Light*, no. 47.

II.40.4 <u>I shall be torn to pieces</u>: the ordeals that Mary, accused of adultery, would face are vividly portrayed in the narrative poem on Joseph and Mary, lines 146–160 (see previous note).

III. Mary and the Magi

III.3.1 <u>the Peoples</u>: early Syriac writers frequently refer to Gentiles as 'the Peoples', and to Jews as 'the People'.

III.7.1 Assyria (*Athor*): Athor denotes the geographical area around Mosul (Syriac: Ninwe, Niniveh).

III.27.2 the Ancient of days: according to the original Aramaic of Daniel 7:13, followed by the standard Greek and the Peshitta, the Ancient of days is differentiated from the 'son of man'. Thus most Christian writers (including Ephrem) associate the Ancient of days with the Father, and not the Son. The Old Greek translation of Daniel, however, speaks of the 'son of man' being '*like* the Ancient of days', thus making it possible for some Christian writers (including the present author) to identify the Ancient of days as Christ. For further details, see Brock, S.P. "The Ancient of Days: the Father or the Son?" *The Harp* 22 (2007): 121–30.

III.34.4 sweet cluster: this term, based on Isaiah 65:8, is rather frequently used with reference to Christ in early Syriac literature, and Aphrahat devotes the whole of his 23rd Demonstration to it.

III.45.2 Lord of the heights: this title of Christ is already found in Ephrem, *Madroshe* on the Crucifixion 5:17, 8:15.

IV–V. MARY AND THE GARDENER

IV.2.2 my Son: the identification of the Mary in John 21:11–17 as Mary the mother of Jesus, is not infrequent in Syriac liturgical poetry; see Murray, R. *Symbols of Church and Kingdom: a Study in Early Syriac Tradition*, 146–8, 331–2. London/Piscataway NJ, ²2004, and for Greek writers, Gianelli, C. "Témoignages patristiques en faveur d'une apparition du Christ ressuscité à la Vierge Marie." *Revue des Études Byzantines* 11 (1953): 106–19, and Aubineau, M. *Les homélies festales d'Hesychius de Jérusalem*, I, 13–15. Studia Hagiographica, 59; 1978.

IV.15.2 Sheol the devourer: the epithet is quite frequently found in liturgical poetry, and perhaps offers some support to D.W. Thomas's suggestion that Belial derives from the root bl^c 'to devour, swallow up': see his "Belial in the Old Testament." In Birdsall, J.N., and R.W. Thomson, eds. *Biblical and Patristic Studies in Honour of R.P. Casey*, 11–19. Freiburg i/B, 1963.

IV.21.2 his mother gives witness to his resurrection: Ephrem, Commentary on the Diatessaron XXI.21 describes the sealed tomb as witnessing to the seal of Mary's virginity. The correlation between Mary's womb and Christ's tomb is common in later liturgical poetry.

IV.23.2 Mary, Mary: in John 20:16 Mary's name is only given once, but the repetition will have been suggested by passages such as Luke 10:41.

IV.24.1 my Master (*rabbuli*): this form, rather than the more familiar *rabboni*, is found in John 20:16 in both the Old Syriac Gospels and the

Peshitta. Ephrem already takes it up as a term of endearment in his *Madroshe* (on the Resurrection 2:5; on the Church 22:2; on Nisibis 6:5).

IV.26.2 <u>on him who composed this</u>: self-reference to the author is a characteristic of several of the later East Syriac dialogue (and other) poems.

V.27.1 <u>you hold sway</u> (*nomê*): the Greek loanword *nomē* already occurs in the Peshitta New Testament, at 2 Timothy 2:17. Although absent from Ephrem, it is employed a number of times by both Narsai (e.g. ed. Mingana, I, p. 348; II, p. 46) and Jacob of Serugh (e.g. ed. Bedjan, I, p. 475; II, p. 132). It caused problems here to some later copyists, who substituted *nugro*.

SELECT BIBLIOGRAPHY

(a) *Dialogue and dispute poems*
[for editions/translations of individual poems, see Appendix]

Brock, S.P., ed. *Sughyotho mgabyotho*. Monastery of St Ephrem, Holland, 1982.

___. "Syriac dialogue poems: marginalia to a recent edition [= *Sughyotho mgabyoto*]." *Le Muséon* 97 (1984): 29–58.

___. "Syriac dispute poems: the various types." In Reinink, G.J., and H.L.J. Vanstiphout, eds. *Dispute Poems and Dialogues in the Ancient and Mediaeval Near East*, 109–19. Orientalia Lovaniensia Analecta, 42; 1991. [Reprinted in *From Ephrem to Romanos: Interactions between Syriac and Greek in Late Antiquity*. Aldershot, 1999, chap. VII].

___. "The dispute poem: from Sumer to Syriac." *Journal of the Canadian Society for Syriac Studies* 1 (2001): 3–20.

___. "Dialogue and other *sughyotho*." In Chehwan, A., ed. *Mélanges offerts au Prof. P. Louis Hage*, 363–84. Université Saint Esprit de Kaslik, Faculté de Musique, Études, 9. Kaslik, 2008.

Murray, R. "Aramaic and Syriac dispute poems and their connections." In Geller, M.J., J.C. Greenfield and M.P. Weitzman, eds. *Studia Aramaica*, 157–87. Supplement to *Journal of Semitic Studies*, 4; 1995.

Reinink, G.J., and H.L.J. Vanstiphout, eds. *Dispute Poems and Dialogues in the Ancient and Mediaeval Near East*. Orientalia Lovaniensia Analecta, 42; 1991.

(b) Mary in Syriac tradition

Amar, J.P. "Most blessed of all women: devotion to the Mother of God in the Syriac-Maronite tradition." *Diakonia* 34 (2001): 203–12.

Brock, S.P. "Mary in Syriac tradition." In Stacpoole, A., ed. *Mary's Place in Christian Dialogue*, 182–91. Slough, 1982 (reprinted as the Introduction to Hansbury, M. *Jacob of Serug, On the Mother of God*, 1–14. Crestwood NY, 1998).

___. *Bride of Light. Hymns on Mary from the Syriac Churches*. Moran Etho, 6. Kottayam, 1994; revised edition, Kottayam/Piscataway NJ, 2010. [This also includes the first four dialogues of the present collection].

Brock, S.P. "Mary and the Angel, and other Syriac dialogue poems." *Marianum* 68 (2006): 117–51.

Budge, E.A.W. *The History of the Blessed Virgin Mary and the History of the Likeness of Christ.* London, 1899. [2 vols, Syriac texts and English translation].

Mar Çiçek, Julius Y. *Tash'itho d-Yoldat Aloho Maryam.* Monastery of St Ephrem, Holland, 2001. [In 6 Books; the third book only was edited, with English translation, by Mingana, A. *Woodbrooke Studies* III, 1–92. Cambridge, 1931, under the title "Vision of Theophilus"].

Gharib, G., ed. *Testi Mariani del primo millennio*, IV, *Padri e altri autori orientali.* Rome, 1991, pp. 45–307: West Syriac texts; pp. 311–437: East Syriac texts; pp. 441–532: Maronite texts.

Hansbury, M. *Jacob of Serug, On the Mother of God.* Crestwood NY, 1998.

Harvey, S.A. "On Mary's voice: gendered words in Syriac Marian tradition." In Martin, D.B., and P. Cox Miller, eds. *The Cultural Turn in Late Antique Studies. Gender, Asceticism and Historiography*, 63–86. Durham NC, 2005.

Hurst, T.R. "The transitus of Mary in a Homily of Jacob of Serug." *Marianum* 52 (1990): 86–100.

Madey, J. *Marienlob aus dem Orient.* Paderborn, 1982. [Translations from the Syrian Orthodox Shehimo, or Weekday Prayer].

Mullassery, M. "Mary, the Blessed Virgin Mother, in the East Syriac Liturgy of Hours." *Ephrem's Theological Journal* (Satna) 8 (2004): 151–67.

Murray, R. "Mary, the Second Eve, in the early Syriac Fathers." *Eastern Churches Review* 3 (1971): 372–84.

Pathikulangara, V. *Mary Matha: the "Divine Praises" for the Feast Days of the Blessed Virgin Mary according to the East Syriac or Chaldeo-Indian Liturgical Heritage.* Denha Services, 49. Kottayam, 1998.

Payngot, C. "Homily of Narsai on the Virgin Mary." *The Harp* (Kottayam) 13 (2000): 33–7.

Pinnock, J. *Fire and Spirit in her womb. Mary in the poetry oif St Ephrem.* Ecumenical Society of the Blessed Virgin Mary, pamphlet, 2003.

Prieto, A.M. "La Theotokos en las Dissertationes de Filoxeno de Mabbug." *Marianum* 44 (1982): 390–424.

Puthuparampil, J. *The Mariological Thought of Mar Jacob of Serugh (451–521).* Moran Etho, 25. Kottayam, 2005.

Shoemaker, S.J. *Ancient Traditions of the Virgin Mary's Dormition and Assumption.* Oxford, 2002. [Much on Syriac texts]

Mar Bawai Soro. *Mary in the Catholic-Assyrian Dialogue. An Assyrian Perspective.* Ecumenical Society of the Blessed Virgin Mary, pamphlet, 1999.

Thykoottam, S. "The typology of Mary in Shima, the weekly Divine Office of the Malankara Church." *The Harp* (Kottayam) 2:1/2 (1989) : 31–44.

Yousif, P. "La Vierge Marie et l'Eucharistie chez saint Ephrem de Nisibe et dans la patristique syriaque antérieure." *Études Mariales* 36/7 (1978/80): 49–80.

———. "Marie, Mère du Christ, dans la liturgie chaldéenne." *Études Mariales* 39 (1982): 57–85.

———. "Marie et les derniers termps chez saint Ephrem de Nisibe." *Études Mariales* 42 (1985): 31–55.

———. "La bellezza di Maria cantata da Efrem di Nisibi." *Theotokos: Ricerche interdisciplinari di Mariologia* 13 (2005): 147–94

APPENDIX: DIALOGUE *SUGHYOTHO*

The list below provides an inventory of all the dialogue *sughyotho* which are at present known, together with their main editions and (where available) translations. The following abbreviations are used:

Feldmann = Feldmann, F. *Syrische Wechsellieder von Narses*. Leipzig, 1896, cited by number. Syriac texts and German translations.

Mingana = Mingana, A. *Narsai Doctoris Syri Homiliae et Carmina*, II, 366–411. Mosul, 1905, cited by number. Syriac texts only.

SM = Brock S.P., ed. *Sughyotho mgabyotho*. Monastery of St Ephrem, Holland, 1982. Syriac texts only. Details of the early manuscript sources used for this edition can be found in "Syriac dialogue poems: marginalia to a recent edition." *Le Muséon* 97 (1984): 29–58.

The brackets after each topic denote the manuscript tradition(s), East Syriac (E) and/or West Syriac (W), in which the *sughitho* in question is transmitted. An asterisk (*) denotes that the text and translation are to be found in the present volume.

OLD TESTAMENT

Cain and Abel, I (E/W)
Cain and Abel, II (E)
   Critical edition of I and II, with English translation and notes: Brock, S.P. "Two Syriac dialogue poems on Abel and Cain." *Le Muséon* 111 (2000): 333–75. Earlier editions of I: Feldmann, VI; Mingana, VI; *SM*, 1; *Qolo Suryoyo* 26 (1982): 27–31.

Abraham, Sarah and Isaac (W)
   Editions: Kirschner, B. "Alphabetische Akrosticha in der syrischen Kirchenpoesie." *Oriens Christianus* 6 (1906): 44–69 (with German translation); *SM* 2. English translation and notes: Brock, S.P. "Syriac poetry on biblical themes, 2. A dialogue poem on the sacrifice of Isaac (Gen. 22)." *The Harp* 7 (1994): 55–72.

Joseph and Potiphar's Wife, I (W)
Joseph and Potiphar's Wife, II (E/W)
> Critical edition of I and II, with English translation: Brock, S.P. "Joseph and Potiphar's Wife: two anonymous dispute poems." In van Bekkum, W.J., J.W. Drijvers, and A.C. Klugkist, eds. *Syriac Polemics. Studies in Honour of Gerrit Jan Reinink*, 41–57. Orientalia Lovaniensia Analecta, 170. Leuven, 2007. Earlier edition of I: *SM* 3.

Joseph and Benjamin (E/W)
> Critical edition, with English translation: Brock, S.P. "A Syriac dialogue between Joseph and Benjamin," forthcoming the *Festschrift for R. Ebied*, edited by P. Hill.
>
> Earlier editions: Çiçek, J.Y. *Kapo d-habobe*, 19–21. Monastery of St Ephrem, Holland, 1977; idem, *Tenḥotho d-Tur ʿAbdin*, 156–8. Monastery of St Ephrem, Holland, 1987; *SM* 4.

Job and his Wife (W)
> Edition and translation in preparation.

NEW TESTAMENT

Zechariah and the Angel, I (W)
> Edition: *SM* 5. English translation: Brock, S.P. *Sogiatha. Syriac Dialogue Hymns*, 7–13. Syrian Churches Series, ed. J. Vellian, 11; 1987.

Zechariah and the Angel, II (W)
> The poem is only known in a fragmentary form.

*Mary and the Angel, I (E/W)
> Editions: Maronite *Fanqitho*, 195–201. Rome, 1656; Lamy, T.J. *Sancti Ephraem Syri Hymni et Sermones* II, cols 589–604. Malines, 1886 (with Latin translation); Manna, J.E. *Morceaux choisis de littérature araméenne*, I, 210–16. Mosul, 1901; Feldmann, II; Mingana, II; *SM* 6.
>
> English translations: Brock, S.P. *Bride of Light. Hymns on Mary from the Syriac Churches*, revised edn. Moran Etho, 6. Kottayam/Piscataway NJ, 2009, no. 41; idem, "Mary and the Angel, and other Syriac dialogue poems." *Marianum* 68 (2006): 117–30.

Mary and the Angel, II (E)
> Edition and translation in course of preparation.

*Mary and Joseph (W)
> Edition: *SM* 7. English translations: Brock, in Beshara, R. *Mary, Ship of Treasure*, 83–5. New York, 1988 (abbreviated); idem, "A dialogue between Joseph and Mary from the Christian Orient." *Logos: the Welsh Theological Review* 1:3 (1992): 4–11; *Bride of Light*, no. 42; idem, "Mary

and the Angel, and other Syriac dialogue poems." *Marianum* 68 (2006): 131–8.
*Mary and the Magi (E/W)
Critical edition, with German translation: Beck, E. *Des heiligen Ephraem des Syrers Hymnen de Nativitate (Epiphania)*. CSCO Scriptores Syri, 82/83; 1959, Soghitha IV. Other editions: Lamy, *Sancti Ephraemi Hymni et Sermones*, I (1882), cols 129–44 (with Latin translation); Feldmann, I; Mingana, III; *SM* 8.
English translations: A.E. Johnston, in Gwynn, J. *Selections translated into English from the Hymns and Homilies of Ephraim the Syrian*, 287–9. A Select Library of Nicene and Post-Nicene Fathers, II.13. Oxford/New York, 1898; Brock, in Beshara, *Mary, Ship of Treasure*, 83–5. New York, 1988; *Bride of Light*, no. 43; idem, "Mary and the Angel, and other Syriac dialogue poems." *Marianum* 68 (2006): 139–47.
Herod and the Magi (E)
Edition, with German translation: Rücker, A. "Zwei nestorianische Hymnen über die Magi." *Oriens Christianus* II.10/11 (1923): 33–55, esp. 36–45.
John the Baptist and Christ (E/W)
Critical edition, with German translation: Beck, *Des heiligen Ephraem ... Hymnen de Nativitate (Epiphania)*. CSCO Scriptores Syri 82/83; 1959, Sogitha V.
Other editions, Lamy, *Sancti Ephraemi Hymni et Sermones*, I, cols 113–28 (with Latin translation); Feldmann, III; Mingana, V; *SM* 9.
English translations: A.E. Johnston, in Gwynn, *Selections*, 284–6; Brock, *Sogiatha*, 21–7.
John the Baptist and the Crowd (E)
Editions: Feldmann, IV; Mingana, IV. English translation to appear.
Christ and the Pharisees (E)
Editions: Feldmann, VII; Mingana, VIII.
Christ and the Synagogue (W)
Edition: *SM* 10.
The Sinful Woman and Satan, I (W)
The Sinful Woman and Satan, II (E)
Critical edition of I and II, with English translation: Brock, S.P. "The Sinful Woman and Satan; two dialogue poems." *Oriens Christianus* 72 (1988): 21–62.
Earlier edition of I: *SM* 11.

English translation of I: Brock, S.P. "Satan and the Sinful Woman: a dialogue poem from the Syriac Churches." *Sobornost/Eastern Churches Review* 13:2 (1992): 33–44.

The Two Thieves (W)
Editions: Kirschner, "Alphabetische Akrosticha... ." *Oriens Christianus* 7 (1907) : 260–83 (with German translation); *SM* 12.
English translation: Brock, S.P. "The Dialogue between the Two Thieves." *The Harp* 20 (2006): 151–70.

The Cherub and the Thief (E/W)
Editions: (a) East Syriac recension: Sachau, E. "Über die Poesie in der Volksprache der Nestorianer." *Sitzungsberichte der königlich-preussischen Akademie der Wissenschaften zu Berlin* XI.8 (1896): 179–215, (with German translation and Modern Syriac version); Pennacchietti, F.A. *Il ladrone e il cherubino. Dramma liturgico cristiano orientale in siriaco e neoaramaico*. Turin, 1993, with Italian translation and Modern Syriac versions; Yawsep d-Beth Qelayta, ed. *Turgame w-Takse da-mshammshanutha w-Soghyatha*, 142–7. Mosul, 1926; Daniel d-Beth Benyamin, ed. *Ktaba d-Turgame w-rushma d-Taksa da-mshammshane wd-Bim 'am Soghyatha*, 158–65. Chicago, 1996.
(b) West Syriac recension: *SM* 13; Brock, "The Dispute between the Cherub and the Thief." *Hugoye* 5:2 (2002): 169–93 (with English translation).
Other translations: Graffin, F. "La soghitha du chérubin et du larron." *L'Orient Syrien* 12 (1967): 481–90; Brock, *Sogiatha*, 28–35; Glenthøj, J. "The Church and Paradise—the Robber and the Cherub in dialogue." In Jeppesen, K., K. Nielsen, and B. Rosendal, eds. *In the Last Days: on Jewish and Christian Apocalyptic and its Period*, 60–77. Aarhus, 1994.

Death and Satan (Ephrem, *Carmina Nisibena* 52–54)
Critical edition: Beck, E. *Des heiligen Ephraem des Syrers Carmina Nisibena*, II. CSCO Scriptores Syri, 102/103; 1963, with German translation. Other editions: Bickell, G. *S. Ephraemi Syri Carmina Nisibena*. Leipzig, 1866, with Latin translation; *SM* 15–17. Edition, with English translation, of *C. Nisibena* 53 in Brock, S.P., and G.A. Kiraz. *Ephrem the Syrian: Select Poems*, 155–67. Provo, 2006.
Other translations: J.T.S. Stopford, in Gwynn, *Selections* ..., 206–8. French in Féghali, P., and C. Navarre. *Saint Éphrem, Les chants de Nisibe*. Paris, 1989. Of *C. Nisibena* 52: English in Brock, *The Harp of the Spirit: 18 Poems of St Ephrem*, 70–2. London, 1983; French in Grelot, P. "Un poème de saint Éphrem: Satan et la Mort." *L'Orient Syrien* 3 (1958): 443–52.

Death and Satan, I (W)
>   Edition: *SM* 14. English translation to appear.

Death and Satan, II (E)
>   Edition, with German translation: Edition and German translation: Reinink, G.J. "Ein syrischer Streitgespräch zwischen Tod und Satan." In Reinink, G.J., and H.L.J. Vanstiphout, eds. *Dispute Poems and Dialogues in the Ancient and Medieval Near East*, 135–52. Orientalia Lovaniensia Analecta, 42; 1991. English translation to appear.

*Mary and the Gardener, I (W)
>   Edition and English translation: (see above, V).

*Mary and the Gardener, II (E)
>   Edition and English translation: Brock, "Mary and the Gardener: an East Syriac Dialogue Soghitha." *Parole de l'Orient* 11 (1983): 223–34. Translation also in Beshara, *Mary, Ship of Treasure*, 66–7, and in *Bride of Light*, no. 44.

OTHER TOPICS (IN ALPHABETICAL ORDER)

(a) Personifications

Body and Soul, I (W)
>   Edition: *SM* 20. English translation: Brock, "The dispute between Soul and Body: an example of a long-lived Mesopotamian literary genre." *Aram* 1 (1989): 53–64.

Body and Soul, II (W; *mimro* attributed to Jacob of Serugh)
>   Edition: *SM* 21. English translation: Drijvers, H.J.W. "Body and Soul, a perennial problem." In Reinink and Vanstiphout, *Dispute Poems and Dialogues in the Ancient and Mediaeval Near East*, 121–34.

Body and Soul, III (E/W) (= 'Abdisho', *Paradise of Eden*, XI)
>   Editions: Cardahi, G. *Paradisus Eden. Carmina Auctore Mar Ebed Iso Sobensi*, 56–61. Beirut, 1888; Yawsep d-Beth Qelayta. *Pardaysa da-'den d-sim ..l-Mar(y) 'Abdisho'...*, 52–7. Mosul, ²1928 = Chicago, ³1988. *SM* 22.

Body and Soul, IV (E)
>   Edition: Darmo, T. *Hudra*, I, 367–9. Trichur, 1960.
>   English translation: Brock, "Tales of two beloved brothers: Syriac dialogues between Body and Soul." In MacCoull, L., ed. *Studies in the Christian East in Memory of Mirrit Boutros Ghali*, 29–38, esp. 35–38. Washington DC, 1995 (reprinted in *From Ephrem to Romanos*. Aldershot, 1999, chapter IX).

Cedar and Vine (David bar Pawlos)
   Edition: Dolapönü (Dolabani), F.H. *Egrotho d-Dawid bar Pawlos d-Beth Rabban*, 166–7. Mardin, 1953.
Church and Christ (E)
   Only a fragment of this dialogue is known.
Church and Sion (W)
   Edition: *SM* 18.
   English translation to appear.
Church and Synagogue (W)
   Editions: Kirschner, *Oriens Christianus* 6 (1906): 22–43, with German translation; *SM* 19.
   English translation to appear.
Cup and Wine (E)
   Edition: Shlemon Isho' Hadbeshabba. *Khamis bar Qardahe. Memre w-mushhata*, 218–9. Prisata da-Nsibin, 2. Nuhadra, Iraq, 2002.
Gold and Wheat (E)
   Edition and English translation: in Brock, "A dispute of the months and some related Syriac texts." *Journal of Semitic Studies* 30 (1985): 181–211, esp. 200–4 (reprinted in *From Ephrem to Romanos*. Aldershot, 1999, chapter VIII). Earlier edition: *SM* 24. The poem is attributed to Khamis bar Qardahe in *Khamis bar Qardahe. Memre w-Mushhata*, 197–8.
Grace and Justice, I (W)
Grace and Justice, II (prose)
   These two texts are known only in a fragmentary form.
Heaven and Earth (prose)
   Edition and English translation: Brock, "A Syriac dispute between Heaven and Earth." *Le Muséon* 91 (1978). The Syriac text is reproduced in *Qolo Suryoyo* 9 (1979): 23–6. Part of the dialogue has unaccountably been interpolated into chapter 30 of Isho'dnah's *Ktaba d-Nakputha/Liber Castitatis*.
The Jordan and the Pishon (E)
   Edition and English translation: Brock, "A Syriac dispute poem: the River Pishon and the River Jordan." *Parole de l'Orient* 23 (1998): 3–12.
The Months (E/W)
   Critical edition and English translation: Brock, "A dispute of the months and some related Syriac texts." *Journal of Semitic Studies* 30 (1985): 181–211 (reprinted in *From Ephrem to Romanos*, chapter VIII). Earlier edition: *SM* 23. The poem is (wrongly) attributed to Khamis bar Qardahe in Shlemon Isho' Hadbshabba, ed. *Khamis bar Qardahe*.

Memre w-Mushḥata, 195–6 (there are a number of variants from the manuscripts used in the critical edition).

Virginity and 'Holiness' (Ephrem)
Edition (of Armenian version of lost Syriac original): Mariès, L., and Ch. Mercier. *Hymnes de saint Ephrem conservées en version arménienne*, 41–57. Patrologia Orientalis, 30; 1961, with Latin translation (compare also no. IX, pp. 73–7, where Marriage and Virginity argue, but in uneven blocks of text).
English translation: Mathews, E.W. "St Ephrem the Syrian: Armenian dispute hymns between Virginity and Chastity." *Revue des Études Arméniennes* 28 (2001/2): 143–69.

(b) Individuals

Behnam and Satan (W)
This rare text is to be found in the *Fanqitho d-Qadishe*, copied by Gabriel Aktas (2005), pp. 748–53.

Cyril and Nestorius (E)
Editions: Feldmann, V; Martin, F. "Homélie de Mar Narsès sur les trois docteurs nestoriens." *Journal asiatique* IX.14 (1899): 446–92, esp. 484–92, with French translation in IX.15 (1900): 469–525, esp. 515–524.
English translation: Brock, "Syriac Dialogue: an example from the past." *The Harp* 15 (2002): 305–18 and (slightly revised) *Journal of Assyrian Academic Studies* 18:1 (2004): 57–70.

Elijah of Hirta and the Angel (E)
Edition: Mingana, X.

Helena and the (Jewish) People (E)
Edition: Darmo, T. *Hudra*, III, 723–6. Trichur, 1963.
English translation: in Brock, "Two Syriac poems on the Invention of the Cross." In el-Khoury, N., H. Crouzel, and R. Reinhardt, eds. *Lebendige Überlieferung. Festschrift für H.-J. Vogt*, 55–82, esp. 63–70. Beirut/Ostfildern, 1992 (reproduced in *From Ephrem to Romanos*. Aldershot, 1999, chapter XI).

Marina and Satan (W)
Edition: Hobeika, P., and L. Cheikho. "Vie et Office de Sainte Marine." *Revue de l'Orient Chrétien* 9 (1904): 419–22. Improved edition, with English translation: Brock, "St Marina and Satan: a Syriac dialogue poem." *Collectanea Christiana Orientalia* 5 (2008): 35–57.

Nero, the Soldiers, and Peter (E)
: Editions: Mingana, VII; Bedjan, P. *Acta Martyrum et Sanctorum*, II, 680–686. Paris/Leipzig, 1891.

King Shapur and the Martyrs (E)
: Editions: Feldmann, VII; Mingana, IX; Manna, *Morceaux choisis*, I, 222–227.

INDEX OF NAMES AND THEMES

Adam, I.5, 7, 29; II.15, 16, 45; III,27
angel(s), I.4, 6, 8, 23, 39; II.2, 41; III.42, 43
Assyria, III.7, 52
Beauty, I.3; V.13
bill of divorce, II.33
Church, III Resp., 53
coals of fire, I.14, 16
conception, I.10, 17; II.1, 21, 24, 29
crown, III.11, 13, 22, 23, 33, 35, 40
darkness, III.1-3, 5, 17
David, I.7
destitute, I.10, 42; III.12, 18
East, III.4
Eden, II Resp.; III Resp.
Epiphany, III.4, 53
Eve, I.18, 19; II.15, 16
fire, I.14, 16, 26, 28, 44; II.6, 30, 35; III.25; V.31, 39
flame(s), I.16, 26, 39, 40; III.25
fruit, I.20, 22; II.14, 16, 26; IV.6-9, 11
Gabriel, I.6
garden, IV.4, 5, 7; V passim
glory, (robe of) I.18
Grace, I.13
Herod, III.34, 35
Holy Spirit, I.35, 36
Horeb, II.26
humility, III.19
Isaiah, II.18

Jerusalem, III.36-8
Joseph, II passim
king, III.12, 14, 16, 18, 20, 22, 24, 26, 28, 32
lamb, II.14
letter, I.9
liberty, I.29
light, III.1, 3, 4, 17, 31; IV.26
love, I.1, 25, 35, 43
Magi, III passim
Mary, passim
midwives, II.22
milk, (Mary's) II.3
mystery, I.9, 15; II.34, 42
peace, I.53; II.2; III.50-1; V.41-2
Peoples, III.3, 5
Persia, III.4, 6, 8, 49, 52
poor, I.42-3; II.2; III.9, 12, 14, 16
poverty, I.43; III.13, 15, 24
pregnant, pregnancy, II.3-4, 8, 11, 13, 19
priests, III.38-9
scribes, III.38-9
secret, II.3, 5, 33; III.28, 30, 36, 42, 46
serpent, I.18
Sheol, IV.15
star, III.6, 19, 21, 31, 41, 43, 45, 47-9
sun, I.7
Titles of Christ
    Ancient of Days, III.27
    Beloved, V.1, 3, 11, 16, 17, 39

Cluster of grapes, III.34
Establisher of all, I.7
Fire, I.40, 45
Fruit, I.11; IV.6, 9
Gardener, IV passim; V.5, 12, 39
Guardian of the garden, V.1, 3, 23
Hidden Divinity, I.41
King, III.6, 7 (great), 13, 17, 21, 31, 40, 49 (great)
Light, great, III.5
Lord of all, I.4, 49; II.14, 44; III.11
Lord of his handmaid (Luke 1:38), V.41
Lord of the heights, III.45
Most High, I.7, 13, 17, 53
Power of the Father (Luke 1:35), I.1
Rabbuli, IV.24
Radiance, III.1
Shepherd, V.45
Son of the Bounteous One I.2
Son of God, III.46-8
Son of Mary, IV.25
Son of the Most High (Luke 1:35), III.44
True One (Father), I.19
Virgin's Son, III.8
Sweet Cluster (Is. 65:8), III.34
Titles of Mary
   daughter of poor parents, II.2
   David's daughter, I.7
   Mother of my Lord, I.11
   Second Heaven, I.37
treasure(s). III.9, 10, 14, 15, 22
truth, II.9, 28, 32, 37, 41; III.29, 50; V.38
virginity, I.25; II.3, 10, 21-2
watcher(s), I.36, 42, 52-3; II.8, 30, 42; III.40-1, 44, 48
womb (Mary's), I.1, 2, 17, 21, 40, 41, 50; II.1, 3, 27, 31, 34-6, 38, 44-5; III.2; IV.19

INDEX OF BIBLICAL REFERENCES

Genesis
    2:21-22   II.16
    3:1-7   I.18
    5:4   II.15
    22:13   II.14
Exodus
    3:2   I.45
    17:6   II.26
Numbers
    17:8   II.26
Isaiah
    6:3   I.47
    7:14   II.18
    21:4   II.18
    65:8   III.34
    65:17   I.37
Daniel
    7:13   III.27
Matthew
    1:18   II.3
    1:19   II.33
    1:20   II.42
    1:24   II.42
    2:2   III.6, 31
    2:3   III.34
    2:11   III.8, 9
    2:16   III.36
    26:53   III.24
    28:10   V.44
Luke
    1:28   I.11; II.2; III.44
    1:32   III.44
    1:32-33   III.40
    1:33   III.42
    1:35   I.35; III.46
    1:38   I.36
    1:42   I.11
    1:48   I.48
    24:5   IV.15
John
    20:1   IV.1
    20:15   IV.4, (14)
    20:16   IV.23
Philemon
    2:10   III.23
Colossians
    1:21-22   I.53
Proto-Gospel of James
    19:1   II.22

www.ingramcontent.com/pod-product-compliance
Lightning Source LLC
Chambersburg PA
CBHW051529230426
43668CB00012B/1789